REWIRE YOUR BRAIN

The Secrets to Overcoming Negativity: How to Change Your Mind and Your Life Habits. Discover the Power of Positive Thinking and Develop Mental Toughness for Success in Your Life.

Richard Kim

Richard Kim© Copyright 2019 - All rights reserved.

The content contained within this book may not be reproduced, duplicated or transmitted without direct written permission from the author or the publisher. Under no circumstances will any blame or legal responsibility be held against the publisher, or author, for any damages, reparation, or monetary loss due to the information contained within this book. Either directly or indirectly.

Legal Notice:

This book is copyright protected. This book is only for personal use. You cannot amend, distribute, sell, use, quote or paraphrase any part, or the content within this book, without the consent of the author or publisher.

Disclaimer Notice:

Please note the information contained within this document is for educational and entertainment purposes only. All effort has been executed to present accurate, up to date, and reliable, complete information. No warranties of any kind are declared or implied. Readers acknowledge that the author is not engaging in the rendering of legal, financial, medical or professional advice. The content within this book has been derived from various sources. Please consult a licensed professional before attempting any techniques outlined in this book. By reading this document, the reader agrees that under no circumstances is the author responsible for any losses, direct or indirect, which are incurred as a result of the use of the information contained within this document, including, but not limited to, errors, omissions, or inaccuracies.

Table of Contents

Introduction

Chapter 1: Rewiring Your Brain

   How to Rewire Your Brain for Success

   Rewire Your Brain by Taking in the Good

Chapter 2: Change Your Mind and Your Life Will Follow

   Reap Financial Benefits by Changing Your Mind

   Way of Disciplining Your Mind

Chapter 3: The Psychology behind Changing Your Life

   Visualizing Your Thoughts

   Stop Focusing on the Negative

Chapter 4: The Law of Attraction through the Power of Your Mind

Discovering the Strength to be Efficient with Positive Thinking

Some Techniques for Positive Thinking

Chapter 5: When Does Positive Thinking Become Dangerous?

Transform Your Life Through Your Habits

How to Live a Healthy Life with Good Habits

Chapter 6: Refection of Bad Habits

The Secret of Building Mental Resilience

What is Mental Toughness

Chapter 7: Mental Toughness—High Frustration Tolerance

Living a Healthy Life

Secrets of Cultivating a Positive Mind-Set

Chapter 8: Ordinary Consciousness or Mindlessness

How to Stop Taking on Negativity from Others

Programming Your Subconscious Mind

Conclusion

Introduction

This book explains that working through any doubts emerging about Ascension is simply part of the process that allows you to ascend. Moving through your worries rewinds your brain-which allows you to ascend.

Did you realize that positive experiences appear to be fleeting rather than negative? You might have a fantastic holiday or talk beautifully and get great feedback, but your mood has darkened the next day. On the other hand, when you make a mistake in public and underestimate a client, you probably stress that for a much longer time. This inherent brain bias is important from a survival perspective of focusing on the negative. Those of our mammalian ancestors who were calm and concentrated on the good in life were eaten by predators rather than the anxious ones, who were constantly searching for danger. Primates who knew what was dangerous and trained their young people to worry about danger, succeeded better in transmitting their genes. The good news is that a simple routine will gradually rewire your mind to replace your negative impulses with a constructive inclination.

Sometimes even the slightest snafu could drive us out of the room storm, reach a mobile, or simply shut down completely. The way to manage our frustration and knee jerk responses is by redirecting our focus to another outcome or possibility. It binds our brain and makes a new neuronal connection - a positive change connection!

Chapter 1:
Rewiring Your Brain

There are not many of us who can say that we have come out of our adolescence unscathed or had some fairy-tale ties. We all have had bad things happen to us. Some of them are worse than others. All too often, we constantly revisit those negative memories to form part of our entire mental structure. After all, all you do is driven by how you look at your history.

Don't you think it's true? If you always fight with weight, cash, and/or love, it's a clear indication that the driver's seat is your history!

Want more evidence? Think about a dream you've got. It could be going back to school, getting away from Mr. or Ms. Wrong, and quitting the dead-end job at last. When you imagine this, what happens? Things pop up everywhere to keep you from advancing. You can't even go beyond the thinking process or even attempt to create a better life.

You can feel scared, indignant, puzzled, depressed, or even anxious. You come up with many reasons not to be content. This is your history, which guides you. These are all the bad, twisted people you have met all your life, who have been able to program your brain.

Exercise: Reprogramming your subconscious. Right now, try to dwell on your negatives. All that does is bring down your power and fill you with an aura that prevents something better from entering your life.

1. Whenever a negative thought about the past comes up, say the word "stop!" or imagine a referee blowing a whistle, something that breaks the well-worn neural path grooves. Sometimes a song that I can sing as loud as I can, can instead be sung softly and gently. Your goal here is to control your unconscious consciously.

2. Once this pattern has been disrupted, replace it with a constructive and equally powerful memory. For example, claim that you have been abused as a child, and a certain incident comes to mind. Bring up a happy memory, instead of entering the memory, and remember it as much as possible.

3. If you don't have many happy memories or find it difficult to find anything when anger or pain strikes, list some happier times when your mood is good and read this list when you feel down. Until I could change my mind, I would read my list five times a day or more.

4. You can even write down things that you expect to attend to in the future. Write down what you need for your next relationship if you were in a really bad relationship. (Be fair though, because nobody's perfect!) Write down what your future colleague will be and share with him/her some happy times. This is also a great way to configure your mind and resources to attract what you want the most.

The past is gone, it's gone. The only way it can influence you now is to let it happen. Such "poor memory" paths have evolved in your brain so that you can remember them much easier—whether we like them or not. Choose to reprogram your subconscious and see how it affects your mood and life.

How to Rewire Your Brain for Success

Scientists have discovered that denying an individual the possibility to get to their 'right' limbs makes the brain more likely to find an alternative path... a rewire!

You can see that everything is still in order on the moving side (it is ready), but the signals or messages from the brain don't transfer due to the damage the stroke has caused.

I can't even imagine how exhausting this has to be for the victim, but the best part is that it has an incredible 95% Taub Center's success rate!

Why do the "Better" Limbs tie-up?

Easy, our brains always take the EASIEST path!

I didn't say the "most advantageous path to you," but instead the most convenient!

The easiest route for the individual suffering from a stroke is the existing routes or the strongest wiring.

As a coach, this is a great example of "Use it, or lose it." And this "easy way" is not just for stroke patients, our brains try the easiest and simplest path always!

Could this be why we can easily write down our goals; however, achieving them is (usually) considered harder than writing them down? Why do some of us set a goal or follow a specific path and use the old patterns and habits so quickly?

What is needed?

The brain wires, shut down the old roads, and power up new routes instead.

How do you go about doing that?

Well, we're going to get to that.

For instance: imagine someone sitting in a car and not being able to drive. You know it doesn't work yet, because your mind doesn't "cord," or "know" how to drive a car!

The brain must first learn the information, wire it deeply, and only afterward, the brain knows how to perform and send messages to various parts of the body and ask it what to do.

What about someone who set the goal of losing weight? It can be achieved; they have the energy, the money, and the capability (they have proof, they likely have already a part of the wiring in place, if they have been around anyone who has lost weight). As the brain hasn't rewired itself, food is the easiest way!

What about fear? Always (I would tell most of us) do all we can to avoid things we are most afraid of, which makes sense, and first, we must deconstruct the old wiring!

The bizarre thing is that we all know that doing what you are most afraid of is a way to deconstruct the wiring of fear!

Why? You're going to create the new way (new program), and you're going to rewire your mind.

How about a career change? Mostly again, they take the easiest route and they do that which is a simpler or more convenient thing, not because they have no capacity to do something else, but because we have not yet created a new road.

That is why many change their 'work' rather than their profession! Same crap, different wallpaper!

That is why our confidence levels are rising and dropping. We have wiring that we believe are actually not in existence. The objective is to make the path to the most confident part of you the strongest, thus creating a path to overcome all others.

You must be the dominant cable, and you must be the most comfortable.

Think deeply about it, everywhere you can see this happening.

For some people who lose weight, they can take a great leap (perhaps Gastric Bypass Surgery, for example) and take the easiest way out of their life (eat), so the brain will rewire itself.

For some people who depend on drugs and alcohol, taking the easiest path is not to avoid but to consume and have easy access to substances, even living in an area that is forbidden from being used for months.

What about a fear-filled life? Fears are the only thing that can mask millions of fears. I recently worked with someone afraid of never being loved by another important person. How is that rewired? We can't create or ask a person to love us: can we revive fear?

What about the fear of never "dying with regret, making something of our lives?"

Essentially, is it easier to rewire the inner worries, restricting thoughts, convictions, and habits?

I have to say no; they aren't more difficult.

Whatever we may want, we should know that the brain prefers the easiest way. That is to say, "it's just too hard to redirect," we might not say it, it's more "I tried to do it, but it didn't work" maybe "I failed" or "I'm just not good enough."

So how do we create new routes? How?

Can you use counseling, hypnosis, advice, CBT, NLP?

Can you find someone with the same wiring as you? We all know the easiest way of overcoming depression, or phobias is doing exactly what we really fear, like the people above who had had strokes, their counselors (the higher you agree that your cabling is wrong, the stronger it becomes, making it harder to rewire. You didn't like someone all that much, and before you know it, you dislike them with passion?) But they had no choice but to drive pain and fear through.

A feeling here. Here is a thought.

It is a case of breaking it down, piece by piece to deconstruct anything. Take one of your fears. What evidence do you have that the fear is wired?

Imagine yourself carrying out the terror that you once had.

Continue to play the picture over and over.

Only look, think, listen, be effective.

What are you doing? Just reorder. The new track models.

Were you ready to create and build a motivated life for yourself? Would you like to reboot your mind for success?

Are you ready to grow in self-confidence, concentrate, and move forward? Do you need some assistance?

Let's do it!

Rewire Your Brain by Taking in the Good

Have you noticed that positive experiences seem fleeting rather than negative? You may take a fabulous holiday or speak brilliantly and have wonderful reviews, but your mood declines the next day. On the other hand, when you make an error in public or confuse a client, you probably stress on this for much longer than that.

This normal brain bias is important from a survival point of view to the negative. Those who were relaxed and dedicated to the pleasant things of our mammalian ancestors were more likely to be eaten by predators than by those who were nervous and always looking for danger. Primates, who knew what was risky and told their young people that they were worried about the danger, had more success in passing on their genes.

The good news is that a very simple practice will rewire the mind regularly, to replace your negative bias with a positive bias. A neuropsychologist and Buddhist educator, co-author of the Brain of Buddha and writer of Hardwiring Happiness, created this method.

You might have heard the sentence "Neurons that fire together wire." This means that neural roads are frequently used to develop stronger connections. Our positive and negative experiences shape our neural habits throughout our lives.

For example, if you had trauma in your childhood, as a part of your emotional state, you probably face background anxiety. On the other hand, when you meditate every day, you will probably experience a strong area of silence in the backdrop of your emotional state.

The practice of Rick Hanson "Take into the Good" leads your brain to a basic state of enjoying the wealth available to us. Recent discoveries like this are great because brain scientists have discovered shortcuts that take years of treatment or coaching to make changes.

Here are the steps: Set aside 5 minutes.

Choose something that will make you happy right now. You might be loved by people who are special to you. It might be that you have a great meal scheduled for this evening or that you are paid for your work. Even if you are sick or injured, you should concentrate on your physical body's harmonious functioning.

Focus your attention for at least 20 seconds on this positive experience.

That's it! It's that straightforward. If you are like most of us, the mind wanders and resists concentrating on a positive experience. But what this 20-second period does is to allow the brain time to savor what is great from short-term memory to long-term memory and to learn from it.

Remember that there is a difference between a 20-second brief positive experience and a 20-second emphasis on savoring the outcome of the experience. That is what makes all the difference in the world that enables you to build your inner state on a positive basis. With this optimistic foundation, the resources are more fully available to you for a change. You may have found this benefit already if you have a practice of appreciation.

Try it! This takes only five minutes at a time. If you regularly invest in this easy practice and become curious about anything that can block it, the results can change your life. Let me know if it works. Let me know tomorrow.

Chapter 2:
Change Your Mind and Your Life Will Follow

We all go about to show that we are good, lovable, talented, and beautiful because we think we are useless, unloved, incompetent, and hideous.

When we feel so nervous about these values, we focus specifically on our fears and desires. We train our senses to discover proof of what we wished to be. It's the act of seeking to disprove our fears, and we are shameful because we want to be just as good as anybody else. The negative convictions cause us to focus our efforts on the areas of life that could show that our convictions are untrue.

Unfortunately, our negative attitudes focus heavily on evidence of what we believe.

For instance, we can get 100 positive comments on who we are in a day, but if we feel we're ugly, we get distracted and remember the only negative comment. It makes us forget all the positive comments and minimize them.

To fix our negative beliefs, we need to live through a void to nothingness, and the nothingness is important to lose control of what we now believe to be true, which makes us fearful that all the negative things we believe to be true about us are true.

It's like the night that brings a fresh day. The night is dark and cold and frightening, but the sun rises bright and warm in the morning.

It takes courage to permit nothing to fill our lives, and it takes confidence to change our faiths. As we don't understand or observe our normal ups and downs, our mind begins to reflect on this moment as it happens.

We can have the courage to face our faith, we can know it, and we can put it down as we picked it up.

We will begin to believe that our beliefs are wrong and that our minds must cleanse itself.

If we stop drinking from the well of what we believe to be true and renew our confidence over and over, we die as grass does when it does not get water.

Be guided by nothing, and since nothing leads us, we have the chance to see our world without our belief in control.

In the dizzying twist of trying to keep things from happening a certain way, all of our energy focuses on trying to keep our negative beliefs from being achieved.

We try and try to make our lives bearable under the burden of what we are afraid of, and build our expectations based on what we think we can or can't do and are helpless in our own life.

In other words, if our lives were to only look like this, we would be happy and loved if we had all these things.

We never try to receive evidence that we are evil, gross, hideous, wrong, and not good enough and to receive good proof that we are fine, beautiful, holy, right, or competent. And everything is based on our negative beliefs about our lives and ourselves.

We live in a stressful world trying to feel secure, safe and cherished, and as much as we try, it's always an emotional rollercoaster.

If we had enough proof that shows us we are good enough, then we would see our lives and ourselves as wonderful and happy.

If we had enough proof that shows us we are not good enough, we would see our lives and ourselves as not good, and instead, we are, therefore, evil.

I'll tell you now.

"Can we live from another collection of convictions that could lead to a new view of ourselves and the world?"

What if everything that happens before our eyes, enters our ears and touches us, means nothing?

What if all the events in our day are isolated events that can be examined individually and not be associated with meaning about our lives or us.

Such activities only become a collection of unconnected events that are entirely attended.

How about not naming, classifying, finding, knowing, avoiding, or attracting? What does this occurrence mean in the past, present, and future, and what can we do to raise or decrease the number of events when this happens in our lives?

Can this be our source of stress, anxiety, and frustration?

How much more energy, gifts, cognitive precision, harmony, calmness, happiness, joy, and love would we have if we could only do what was needed, completely present in this moment.

Here's the problem.

We tend to see that our convictions reconstruct by seeing confirmation of what we believe.

This is the only problem with our way of thinking.

If we truly believe that we are ugly, indignant, evil, hideous, not good enough, incompetent, unresponsive, cruel, or incapable, it is because we believe it is true, it goes on, without doubt, it does not look, and it becomes invisible.

In other words, it becomes who we are, and the bad trust must now be compensated because it is true to us.

Such truly negative beliefs based on the 5-year-old's expectations and feelings are what we want to do and what we are trying to change.

What we want is the opposite of these negative convictions.

Only placing our negative beliefs is what we don't want and asking us what we want for ourselves and to our lives.

So, everything is founded on negative convictions so that all negative views are more real and true to us.

It's a total pit before you hear something like that.

Read this until you can begin to see how your convictions make your life the way it is. Then start questioning your beliefs deeply. You will see that what you think is regulated, can instead influence what you believe.

In this instance, you might begin to do this if you genuinely believe it has anything possible. What you say and think is now what you believe.

Could you change your mind?

Reap Financial Benefits by Changing Your Mind

Two kinds of people exist in life. Some produce and consume products and services; and others hire and those who are employed; some sell and who buy. Those with wide-open eyes expect a chance to help them improve their fortunes, and those with a celestial eye expect a deliverer to come and save them.

Lifetime consumption is expensive, and people who produce products and services, have to pay for their ideas. The "prosumers" - producers and consumers - must be our own. Consumption is nothing right. At one point or the other, we all consume. The problem arises when you have nothing to give to other people for their lifetime use. For example, reading this chapter is another type of consumption. The ideas and details in this section are all relevant.

I believe that people should learn to obtain skills and knowledge and then use the skills and knowledge gained to their advantage. Bear in mind that not everybody is a businessman. Organizations that care for their employees will always have recruitment strategies in place to retain their best skills. This is most frequently achieved through the introduction of opportunities to this talent pool that may include benefits, such as involvement in the company. After a time of loyal, dedicated, and positive service to the organization, many businessmen leave the organization. Motivated and experienced businessmen will not abandon companies due to the impact on subordinates. We will leave because they have had time to listen to the call for imagination and freedom in which they govern their destiny.

People make lives that are affected by many factors driven by the value of the opportunity - choosing to sacrifice one chance for the other. Such decisions will be guided, for example, by fear of the unknown (risks), know-how, security (assurance that the sun will rise tomorrow), and comfort - knowing what to do and how to do it. The reality is that in fact, there are no assurances. We must learn to let things go in order to gain better and bigger things. If your call is not entrepreneurship, don't push it and be frank with yourself. If you work, keep working exceptionally well, develop yourself, and prepare to climb the ladder of the company. Draw plans and methods for the creation of personal wealth.

Financial literacy does not mean to make much money, but to keep it after making it. Regrettably the majority of education systems worldwide are designed to produce workers for life rather than employers. Such countries can be easily recognized by looking at their unemployment and poverty rates. Even those of us who say we are educated, cannot innovate or come up with ideas for producing products that can create jobs.

The ability to understand why and learn from things is an ability to survive and overcome economic difficulties. The mental preparation and ability to know would help you become a smart, prosperous, and successful businessman, entrepreneur, or shareholder. It defines a group of people who realize that they do not study for money when they work full-time jobs. You understand the value of investing in technology and the return of such investment. Once they have acquired sufficient knowledge, they search for possibilities to apply the information.

Many people start the wrong way with the right thing. With the aid of experts, people in this group may reduce the risk of starting their own businesses or taking quantum leaps to create or expand their investment portfolios. Many people in this group are happy, have a positive attitude towards life, and think positively. Individuals in this group are ready to sacrifice a share to gain more, and are still looking for opportunities for trade or investment.

We were all created with a powerful tool known as 'will.' We use our will to accept or reject any call to do something and approve or disagree with how things are done. The Creator can't veto our will. Life is encouraging all of us to know daily. You can see, life knows that we all have the power, the strength, and the desire to be good. It is the type of learning that cannot be acquired, found, or provided by any learning institution. Life is your best teacher, and he can teach you well if you allow him to—only if you are willing, ready to learn, and available.

Those in this group know that failure in the learning curve is temporary and an opportunity for adding credits. I believe strongly that failure inspires only winners, as losers are defeated. Those in this group who allowed their lives to teaching and were sufficiently patient to complete their course are wiser and mature. The desire to learn helps people in this group learn to own things and not allow things to dominate them. You humbly accept that God and the Cosmos graciously rewarded you. We understand the value and significance of emotional intelligence. We have built our thoughts and eyes to consider, conceptualize, and see what ordinary people can see and so create a way to survive and, more importantly, seek money-making opportunities where people have given up hope. People in this group understand that they must not only dream but also believe and act on strategies to acquire knowledge to achieve great things. I understand that the best investment I can make is to invest in information about the values of financial freedom and the creation of wealth. In making action plans, they provide a strategy that will help them achieve their dreams.

If you hope for the big break that fixes all your money problems, you're going to spend the rest of your life miserable. This kind of mentality leads you to blame all but yourself for your economic misfortunes and problems. You would blame all problems on a government, the economic structure, and other citizens, and prospective employers. In this category, most people are afraid to take initiatives or ask for information and ideas. They have acknowledged their conditions somehow and become impotently stuck. When you work, you can spend most of your best years working hard for money and never really get enough. If you don't work, you spend most of your time worrying not about what you can do to improve your situation, but what your governments or people can do to help you.

Most people in this group are cynical, dismissive of themselves and their environments, and blame other people for what they are doing. A psychological structure is such that we are unable to do something better for ourselves anywhere. We blame our current circumstances for our trauma; where we have shut ourselves up in the past because we cannot accept it beyond the present to move forward into the future. The effect of such a mental framework is that we, who own and sustain it, disempower ourselves by constantly drawing an example of our boring lives. We prefer to always worry about something or someone while the optimist expects challenges, and the realist changes the sails ready to sail in tempestuous seas.

Failure is not a failure until it is acknowledged through a change of direction or abandonment. Nothing and nobody will stop you forever if you permit it. It should be noted that not all failure is bad; many lessons could be learned from it. We should start by asking ourselves the following questions: What do I want to do with my life?

Does it need special skills? What will I do to acquire these skills?

Where am I heading for assistance?

Definitely intended, people want to do something with their lives. This must be the end. Most people from this group are honest, hardworking people, but they can work for the rest of their working lives without basic financial knowledge – financial literacy – and they have very little, if anything.

The best way to get out of your current financial situation is to search for your life and find its purpose. We all have the potential and the strength to be successful and do anything we want to accomplish. Living a life of financial freedom is a challenge involving a willingness to learn, develop, and improve financial literacy skills in the adoption and application of financial strategies leading to financial freedom.

You could have to search your heart and analyze your belief systems more carefully, particularly lessons that counter to your desire to gain financial knowledge and wealth. Delete from your process any negative prospects of wealth and finance and continue to seek information. Start with what you have (skills, experience, and time) and use it to create a seed you planted for knowledge acquisition. Everything planted must germinate, grow, and produce fruit. So, it is important to invest in your knowledge. Because of a lack of knowledge, people cannot live their potential. Knowledge is power, and the absence of it kills people.

Way of Disciplining Your Mind

Mental discipline has always been one of the major human issues. The problem in the modern material world has become much harder when the mind is diverted numerously. During childhood, it is hard for a child to concentrate on his studies; the need for mental discipline is felt. Once he starts reading a textbook, his mind turns to other things, and he loses focus. As a consequence, even after spending hours, he does not understand and remember the substance of the subject. Nonetheless, a good student has no difficulty concentrating his mind on the subject and can learn a lot more at the same time.

The problem of the wavering mind does not end with the human being growing. Many people find it difficult to focus on the task ahead, even in their youth and later years. Their mind is full of thoughts that seem to come and go without the person's control. Therefore, whenever the individual tries to concentrate his mind on any problem, random thoughts interrupt his mind, and he begins to think about other problems rather than the problem in hand. Yet even though the other thought will not last long, the mind will soon be flooded with yet another thought, and the second problem will be dismissed without a solution to the problem.

A person who has no control over his thoughts is filled with many unsolved problems that continue to trouble him as soon as his mind finds some peace. The many challenges make him anxious and nervous. Often in the evening, he loses his sleep as soon as he goes to rest. The unresolved problem begins to disturb him.

Most people need peace of mind, as a restless mind cannot live in peace and happiness.

Mind-control strategies. We learn many ways to control our minds. Meditation is the most common among them. Here, we try to concentrate our minds on an object or idea for long hours and avoid the other thoughts. Nevertheless, it is impossible for most people to control their emotions during meditation. Yes, the more they try to concentrate their minds on anything, the more thoughts that stream like water through his mind when the floodgates are open.

Some people try to concentrate their minds by isolation. We withdraw for some time in an isolated place to lose contact with the external world. We don't watch television or hear the news, anything that doesn't encourage our minds to respond to any outside thinking.

Vipassana is another common mind control method, meaning to look at things as they are. Vipassana is one of the oldest meditation techniques taught by Gautama Buddha. There are a variety of Vipassana courses that last for 10-15 days. These are performed under the guidance of a professor in Ashram, often far away from the cities. All communications from the outside world are disrupted during the stay, all physical encounters are interrupted, and all prayers, yoga, and others are stopped. Vipassana meditation requires silence and strict control of water.

Yoga is another way to increase the focus of the mind and is nowadays very popular in the West. There are many other courses, including Sri Ravishankar's Art of living, which is very common also for calming the mind and bringing peace to life. Yoga requires the person to exercise certain postures of the body and adopt a disciplined lifestyle free of intoxicants, rewards, etc.

Mind control techniques. The mind control techniques are certainly successful because the Guru believes these techniques are common. Nevertheless, these strategies cannot permanently change a person's life. After the practice of Yoga, Meditation, Vipassana, or Art of Living, every person should return to his normal life. Many people find the life of a yogi or Vipasani impossible to live in real life. The effect is, again, the stimulation of the mind if the individual is facing the real world.

Therefore, it is necessary to understand the true principles behind mind discipline, which a person should obey in his daily life, i.e., during his regular work and in the environment of his office and house. If you do yoga and meditation just minutes a day as a morning exercise, it is impossible that you will have a concentrated mind all day long. As he raises the time used for therapy, it reduces the time he has to do his work, leaving him more impatient.

Mind Control. When we study closely, we will find that the control of the body and senses is the secret to mental control. Gita (III 42-43) describes in the following words the relationship of body, senses, mind, soul, and the supreme spirit (God).

The senses are lower than the brain. The body is above the senses, and the soul is above the mind, and God is above the heart (Universal Intelligence).

Gita further states that all actions are carried out entirely by the man's soul. One who is deluded by his ego feels,

"I am the doer." (Gita, III 27) During body and senses, the command is the secret to mind control. If a man can control his body and senses, his mind must be controlled automatically. If the human mind is in its power, its essential essence is transformed, and it transforms the nature of the person since the physical being is nothing more than the representation of the spiritual soul.

This is why all methods of mental control try to control the person's body and senses. The body is regulated by putting discipline into the man as if he gets up early on a certain day, exercises, does physical activities, etc. The senses are controlled by limiting the input of the eyes, ears, nose, skin, and sexual organs to five senses. The inputs of the senses are governed by silence, and all kinds of repetitive tasks are avoided. The mind of the individual is slowly calmed and centered by the stimulation of the body and senses.

Yet once the individual returns to the real world, his mind is distracted again, as all circumstances artificially created cannot last forever.

Mind for Life Discipline. Once we understand the fundamental principles of mind control, we can exercise them in our daily lives without attending classes or teachers. The training should take place in every waking hour so that it becomes part of our identity as our soul is transformed by the discipline of body, senses, and mind.

Corporal punishment means following a schedule in the morning, eating breakfast, lunch, dinner, and sleeping at fixed times during the night. Except in exceptional situations, you should try to stick to your routine. Physical exercise, yoga, cycling, sports will offer more body discipline that can speed up mind control.

The other task of sense control and body control must be done to achieve the best results. Nose regulation can be accomplished by eating healthy foods and stopping sweet, high-calorie, cold, or meat. You should avoid talking loudly and excessively to regulate your voice. In order to control sound outputs, loud music and voice outputs must be avoided. You need to monitor how you think as every output of audio-video stimulates the brain.

One must, therefore, avoid the inputs, which disturb the peace of mind.

These are not difficult measures, and you can track them easily on a daily basis, whether at home or on your walk. Practicing such control alone can alter the temperament and relax a person's mind, allowing him or her to concentrate and resist body and mind's restlessness.

The secret to mind control is the control of the body and the senses of the self. We can regulate our body and senses, but we don't have any physical way of controlling our mind and thought that transforms our personality. Once the nature of a man has changed, no effort is needed to regulate his mind as his mind calms down and concentrates on having peace and happiness in his life. Someone wisely said, "Whatever you think is going to happen in your life, you will continue to act as you always believed if you continue to believe. If you keep doing as you have always done, you will keep getting what you have always got." All you have to do is change your mind if you want different results in your life or job.

Life is a mystery that neither science nor scripture can describe. Truth has a body and a spirit that we refer to as science and religion. Unlike popular perception, they do not contradict each other, but like body and soul complement each other. Ultimately, they can't exist without each other.

Chapter 3:
The Psychology Behind Changing Your Life

I have read another set of statistics every few months or a report that shows that the majority of people are dissatisfied. About 75% of people appear not to like their work, while a recent survey found that almost 93% of people are concerned about money. But what's your life like never minding the statistics? Want to change your life? Are you someone who is looking for financial freedom? Will you suffer from timidity? Want to be more relaxed, more desirable, more comfortable with yourself? Do you hate your job? Or is it difficult to fit into the dress suit that has returned to fashion?! The truth is that if you were able to get a magic bottle and you had to take three snacks every day, that would change your life, you would be a very wealthy person! It would take almost something like that magic potion though, as the odd thing is, although we all want to change our lives, we are simultaneously afraid of change. That's just how we're wired.

We are habitual people. That's how we're made. We become vulnerable to what psychologists call habitual by the age of 2 months—yes, months, not years. When we become used to somebody or something, we stop paying attention to it—the media has taken away. And when we were two or three years old, we knew the hazards of seeking new opportunities, new situations, and new people. So, as we become 'mature' adults, we tie down, fence in, although I don't know many mature adults. We call it our life—but actually it's about life passes.

One of the key effects of the habit is that we stop paying attention to what we do on a regular basis. Everything becomes normal sooner or later, though, and, in the end, we pay no attention. The research essentially suggests that your ability to be happy and successful—of course, I assume that you want to turn your life into a happy and successful life – is directly related to your ability to pay attention.

The consequence of our failure to pay attention and our repetitive behavior and our belief that there is a risk inherent in new and unknown situations, locks us into an existence that is a pale shadow of the life we should lead. Yet ask the next person how they do, and they're likely to respond, "Not so good truthfully," or "Not so bad." Not too bad is not good enough in my opinion -Why are you frustrated but not unhappy to walk through your life?

You've got a problem, therefore! How will you change your life if you fear change! You shouldn't get upset about this phenomenon—because it's the human condition, it's like us. But that doesn't mean it's the way you have to stay. Why should you live like that if the pleasure and excitement of a fully lived life are before your own eyes if you just go to the trouble of opening them? I already stated that we don't pay attention to anything as normal adults. I also said that focus is related to your happiness. You should relearn the knowledge you used as a child to pay attention to what is really happening here and now.

Have you ever heard the well-known saying you have to stop and smell the roses? Okay, that's just what you have to do. The daily routine tumbles the mind - we wander through a senseless existence. To break this psychological loop, you have to hit your senses. Literally, I mean you really must stop and smell the roses. You really must stop in your tracks—call your attention—and face the wonderful truth that actually happens right in front of you. You must see the chances a numb mind can't see. You should know the sincere joy of a particular moment that the ordinary mind finds a routine in. You must wake up. You must wake up.

If you wake up, or if you wake up, you will know there is no such thing as fear. And you should freely try the change you want in your everyday life. Once you discover it, you know how easy it really is to change your life.

What do I say? What do I mean by this? Okay, your life today is the full product of every little thing that you have done, half-done, or not really completed—going back to the age of eight or nine. Every little thing you ever did in your life brought you to where you now are. The argument is that the little things you do will change your life—not some big scary, frightening-of-life changes you have to make. In other words, there will be nothing to be scared of.

So, here's a quick guide if you want to change your life. Then make small changes. Small changes interrupt your habitude and allow you to begin paying attention to what you do—however, routine, and what you might have felt you did. For example, tonight, you can brush your teeth with the hand you normally don't use. Mess with your brain, you messed up your entire life as an adult—and you were far from in the ideal place. You will find yourself mercilessly—yes, I said without effort—if you come to your senses, pay attention to the little things in your life. Start making larger changes that you would otherwise usually fear. And once you begin to change, you are put in a whole new world, which though will always be there; will instead open your eyes to the possibilities and chances of life.

Visualizing Your Thoughts

If people are interested in majorly changing their life, it can be frightening. Many people are resistant to change because they go through the pain with the transition. I will share a great tip with you, which will turn that perceived pain into the whole opposite—something that instead makes you feel great.

It is known as visualization.

It's one of the most effective ways to radically change your life and instead imagine how you want to live.

I'll give you a warning at the beginning if you are new to this exercise—you might feel uncomfortable the first time. We were brought up in a world where it is typically frowned upon to imagine, to dream, or to fantasize about what we want. How many times can you remember daydreaming at school, and the teacher told you to take care?

But what's wrong with visualizing is that it helps to get you to where you want to be. Kids who daydreamed in school are the same kids who now live the life they dreamed of all those years ago.

Our minds are very powerful. Whenever we have an idea in our mind, it sends our body to the right vibration, and then on that vibration, we act. Our thoughts essentially control our feelings, and our feelings dictate our actions. If you doubt this, look at the economic turmoil that is happening today to so many people. You permitted thoughts of loss and weakness to determine how you felt—lost, confused, and frightened. Now that you are in this unpleasant vibration, you behave in ways that make your life more wanting. You also reduced your expenses. You find yourself in a job, you're unhappy. You can't find a way out because life is missing.

If you didn't feel that terror, you wouldn't be restricted anymore, if you knew that the whole universe was at your fingertips, you would understand that you are responsible for all aspects of your life. You wouldn't be scared of the economy or live in a job you hate. You should know that you only control your life—nobody or anything else. You will know that you own your own money and your own happiness. And you'll think about plentiful, healthy, life-giving ideas, which make you feel these positive emotions and act positively to improve your life.

Have you ever seen in pictures what you think? If we think of anything, we have an image in our minds, and we can see that thought. Think of the automobile you drive, the kitchen in which you eat, or the bed in which you sleep. Think of the inside of a movie theatre, waiting and watching a soccer game at the airport. Those pictures pop into your mind, one after the other; all these things can be seen.

This helps us to use this visualizing ability as we think in images. We may take the picture in our mind literally and turn it into a physical form in our universe.

It's crucial to decide what you want. It must be simple. Otherwise, this exercise will not bring you any good results. Unfortunately, you are probably not going to get any results. You really have to sit down and figure out what you want from life and how you want to live all of it. From the house you want, to the friend you want, to the shoes you are wearing, to your everyday lifestyle—take a few minutes to write it all down—the more detail you give this new life image, the better the results.

Now that you have a clear view of the kind of life in which you want to live, it is majestic glory in everything, and you want to burn this image into your mind. Close your eyes and continue to see the vision you have just written down.

See the difference? In both cases, you put your emotions in the frame, which is important for this exercise. Nevertheless, you only want to express constructive, not negative emotions.

The unfiltered thought is your true desire, while the filtered thought is your desire with restrictions. If the image you visualize starts filtering your desire, it will never manifest because you invest negative emotions and visualize the lack rather than focus on positivity and abundance. So be aware that you start doing this and do not get out of control. Remember, your life is in control.

You must be alone with your thoughts to visualize effectively. This is not to be negotiated. So, turn off all distractions—your phone, your television, your radio, and your screen—anything that lets your mind wander. You don't want to fight to hear what the world wants to give you.

When you think of your new life, feel it all. Feel good. Feel good. Feel the love. Feel the love. Feel happy about everything in your life. If you want a family, feel like you're ecstatic about having a family. If you want to operate your own company, feel the absolute joy that you can earn your own money, do something that you like to do, at your own time.

Most people imagine themselves as they want to be, and that is 100% wrong. You will always manifest a state of becoming when you imagine yourself. You want to imagine as if you are the person now because that is what is going to be created. Remember when you were a kid and thought that you were a world-class athlete or a renowned dancer? That's the same thing.

You'll want to have this exercise at least once a day for a few minutes—twice as much as you can. You can't believe the energy you unleash when you begin to imagine your new life daily.

In order to recap, you must first define clearly what you want. So, see where you are unshaken and truly feel your true, unfiltered love for this new life. When you finish, you will feel your body in a vibration of positivity and happiness. This sound determines what you do, and the results will be collected. You will change your life faster and easier than you ever thought by visualizing it daily.

Stop Focusing on the Negative

If you want to succeed, it is the first thing you want to do to change your mind. You must be SELF AWARE. Stop concentrating on the negatives and focus solely on the positives. If you get angry, you stay mad as you keep thinking of these negative thoughts. Essentially you add more fuel to the fire to make you angrier. People dwell and focus on all the wrong things that happen, but never stop remembering any of the good things that happen. People are pushing themselves harder and harder, but they never stop pushing themselves.

Saying "positive thought" may sound like a cliché, but most clichés appear to be real. Once you have a bad mind, that's the perfect time to catch it, shift your perspective, and change your mind-set.

Whatever you keep trapped in your comfort zone is what you need to change. To change something, you have to do something totally contrary to what your mind tells you. A common example here is that you see people dancing and having fun at a wedding. You want to dance too, but a thought tells you that you would look ridiculous and restrict yourself from doing that. Instead of letting the thought dominate you, remind yourself that you have only one life and that you want to live as your last one. If you believe and feel the raw realities and rationality behind that thinking, your mood and perspective will change. You regain confidence slowly and go back.

You ask yourself and really analyze your own thoughts in order to improve your attitude. Don't think about things but consider whether or not this reasoning is motivated by a logical or autonomous view. If it is an individual view, forget it and focus on the RATIONAL. When you continue to rely on your negative thoughts, you'll question the path to success later. The only way to break a habit is by practicing and trying to change your thinking. Anything in your mind that impedes clear thinking will definitely inhibit your progress.

Understand your goal and set yourself a path

Understand your goal and set yourself a course that motivates everyone to drive. Some have children, others have a family, and some just have their own children. If you are to achieve success, the foundations and steps to reach this ultimate goal must be clearly defined. If you want to change your mind, happiness is the only thing that motivates others to drive themselves harder. We have many meanings and ways of achieving happiness, and I like to believe that the aspirations of everyone should be a much larger purpose than money, even if it includes the "feeling of happiness." If you want to support someone other than yourself, you must set clear financial targets to help you get closer to your humanitarian journey. Life has a far greater purpose, and materialism is not and will never be the answer. Find something which drives you, and gradually, you'll begin to change your mind. This is a true success tool.

Once you have built a framework that motivates and moves you forward, your goals must be clearly defined. How will you get there? Each detail must be drawn up to create a road map to your destination. Your goals must be tangible and rational. Don't force yourself forward. When your goals are formed, just remember that you should always do something PRODUCTIVE. Create daily, weekly, and monthly targets to meet consistently. Set long-term goals to help push you and set short-term deadlines that will keep you on track. Do not rest until these targets are met. You have to create a foundation to change your mind-set, and finding your course is just the beginning.

Sticking to these targets will be the hard part. Keeping it consistent will be the only way you can establish a routine and discipline; the practice you need to change your thinking.

Focusing on the moment

Focusing on the moment is only a natural part of life. The wonder of all that happens at once always inspires me. You have to have a clear mind to succeed. To do this, you do not have to be thinning—actually, process what's happening NOW. If your thoughts do not spread around you, you feel more in touch with reality and yourself. As you think continuously, your mood starts to be influenced by certain emotions or reactions. This prevents your progress from changing negative thinking because a thought usually triggers negativity. Concentrate on your targets and specific objectives to help you get there, and anything else is turning your focus to the moment. The emphasis is on how real inspiration hits, and it is important to change your mind.

Journal

Journaling is the only way to track your progress. You document and recollect what your conscious and subconscious mind is thinking by journaling. When you have heard that you only use 10% of your brain, imagine what you can reveal by journaling. When you journal, your own shortcomings and negative thoughts can be much clearer. If you are conscious, the mind loops various things, and people usually don't have enough interaction with themselves to be aware of each and every thought that crosses their minds. The purpose of the journaling is to see how your thinking responds to certain events and how you can alter the pattern so that you can create another occurrence, circumstance, feeling, or opportunity in the future and change your thinking.

Journaling is very relaxing. You feel clean and much happier after getting it all out since journaling is a form of self-therapy. Write every day and practice coherence, as ultimately, this will allow you to recognize negative habits and discipline.

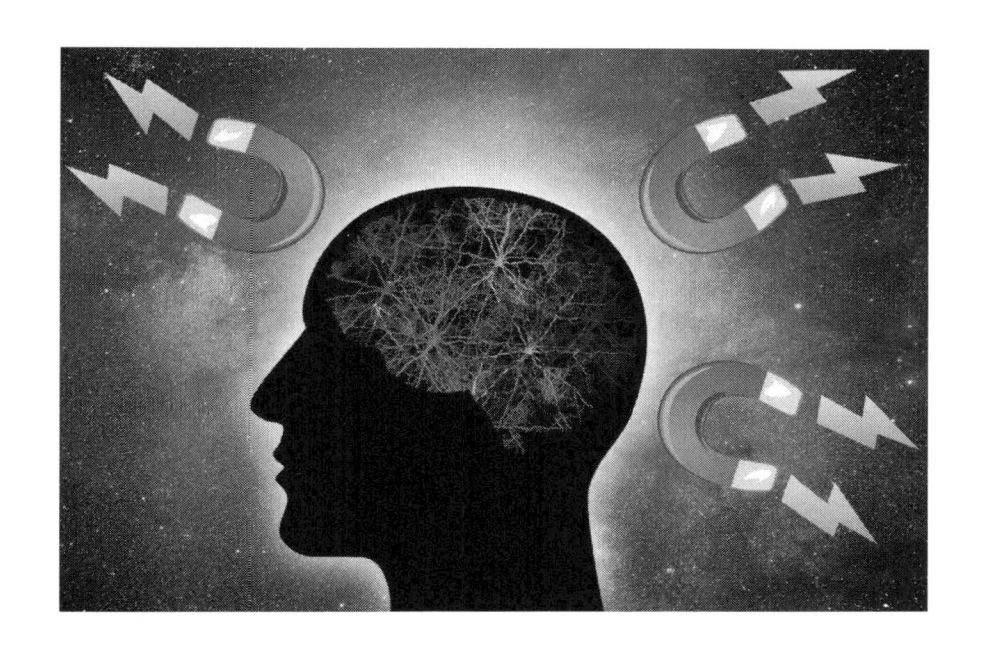

Chapter 4:
The Law of Attraction Through the Power of Your Mind

The Law of Attraction is about using your mind's power to produce outcomes you would not have expected otherwise. It retrains your mind and laser to focus on the things you want in your life. You really are on a winning formula when you have that skill, and then you can intensify them by including the feelings you feel when they come true. You see that your body is made up of energy in its pure form, as James Ray said: "there's a short period of energy sharing a physical body." Then, if you can direct that energy to what you want, you can attract it back to yourself by increasing your vibration or energy that is emitted at any given time.

Many people find it difficult to retrain their minds in this way. Have you ever sat quietly in a chair yourself and tried to focus on one thought for a long time? It is very complicated - you think of other things, some important and others insignificant, but at the end of the day, the outcome is the same. The question is, therefore, how do we train our minds to concentrate on what we want from life?

The first option would be just to replicate the concentration cycle, so it happens all day long. If you have free time, focus on your target with the strength of your mind, and include your emotions when they are achieved. You can also make this process formal by sitting each morning and night quietly for fifteen minutes (to begin with).

The trick to this whole process is not to get frustrated about yourself if your mind wanders but brings it back every time. You will find that you will retrain your mind over time and be able to concentrate on a much longer time than you ever anticipated.

The other way you can improve your concentration and potentially repatriate your mind is to listen to a certain kind of music called isochronic beeps.

The students with "problems" were superior to the control group after using audio-visual brainwave stimulation and significantly increased their grade point average. Perhaps better, even after the test, the GPA for the eight students continued to improve.

We, humans, are still in our infancy when it comes to our brain operations and the incredible power it possesses. I have to confess to being a big Star Trek fan and the iconic words 'space the final boundary' have come to mind, but in this case, I think Gene Rodenberry has been off the scene. Space is not the only barrier, but your mind. As humans, our next goal is to really understand and to start mastering the power of one's mind so that we can use the Law of Attraction to build the lives and environment we all want.

One of the main problems when it comes to our mind is that we are programmed or even 'hard cabled' at a very young age as humans and that hard cables are difficult to change or modify as we get older. It's a bit like a house that must be fully transformed, it's not a simple task, but it needs devastation, a little terror, holes in walls to get to the cable system and much more, but believe me that, once the wiring is done, the journey is well worth it.

We are scheduled for different expectations and values as infants, and they sadly stay with us. For example: so, I am not intelligent enough. Successful people are all greedy, and they have no ethics. These people are different from us—we are working-class people. You can never aspire to this level of greatness. Do not waste your time trying; the only way for you to have all this wealth is to win a lot. Such kinds of assumptions are called restricting convictions that prevent you from pursuing your dreams. The brain is incredibly strong and does not always work for you. You must, therefore, retrain and use isochronic beeps as one way of doing this in a way that is much faster and easier than previously thought. These are sounds that you can activate parts of your brain that you have not previously reached and thus produce instant results.

This technology is truly remarkable, and I would certainly encourage you all to consider using it because it is really effective. The universe will really become your oyster if you can begin to master the power of your mind. It is said that we only use 5% of our mind power when we function at Einstein's capability. From using this technology, we can all start moving into this sphere and break up some of our preconceived ideas that "we are only working-class people, and lifestyles are not there for us."

I'm not thinking just about financial wealth, but about wealth that comes with developing a healthy lifestyle, good connections, and a strong family life. All of it can be there for you, but it takes some time to reprogram your brain to really reach its full potential.

I'm not one that promotes openly other people's goods but looks at MindPowerU's Stephen Pierce. The kit has been a turning point for many people and contains isochronic beeps and other technology that will easily monitor your mental capacity in order, for you to live the life you want.

Good luck on your journey and may today be the beginning of something wonderful for you.

Discovering the Strength to be Efficient with Positive Thinking

Your behavior dictates the status of the "country" in which you reside, i.e., positive results and negative results. It's going to make or break you.

Positive thinking and behavior prepare the brain with feelings, words, and pictures that generate the actions needed for the desired results. Positive mental conduct wants and predicts good and positive outcomes (positive results). An optimistic outlook foresees peace, happiness, wellbeing, and the successful outcome of all circumstances and actions. Whatever the brain wants to do, there is a way to do it.

Despite their lives, a majority of people do not have positive thinking. Not everybody knows this or believes in positive thinking. Many people consider the subject as just nonsense, and others ridicule people who believe in it and support it (e.g., negative behavior that contributes to negative results). Not many people who accept it know how to use it efficiently enough to achieve results. Nevertheless, it seems that many are drawn to this subject, as shown by the numerous books, lectures, and courses. This is a topic that is becoming more popular. The books like "The Key," and "Chicken Soup for the Soul," provide recently good examples to promote a positive thinking process. It's common to hear people say, "think positively!" to someone who feels and cares. Many people don't take these words seriously, because they don't understand or think they actually mean what they say. How many are you aware of, who avoid talking about the power of positive thinking? The challenge for people to embrace this is that we tend to accept negatives better than positives, as a person often needs to battle his natural tendencies.

According to a writer, Mary Lore: "How do we know whether a thought is successful or not?" Basically, by seeing how we feel when we think a thought. We don't feel well when our thought isn't working for us. Our head and neck are tense, and our eyes strained; our breath is shallow, our chest and stomachs heavy. We feel peace. They feel peace. We feel a sense of inner strength.

This is the strength of positive thinking. We feel inspired.

Ashley requested a new job, but because his self-esteem was weak, and he felt he had failed and was incapable of success, he was certain he wouldn't have the job. He had a negative attitude to himself and felt that other candidates were better and more eligible than him. Thanks to his negative experience with job interviews, Ashley displayed this mind-set.

His mind was full of negative thoughts and fears about the position the week before the job interview. He was sure he was going to be rejected. He got up late on the day of the interview and, to his surprise, found that his shirt was dirty and that the other had to be ironed. Since it was too late, he went out with a wrinkle-filled suit.

He was nervous, had a negative attitude during this interview, worried about his jacket, and felt hungry because he didn't have enough time for breakfast. It diverted his mind and made it difficult for him to focus on the interview. His overall attitude had a bad effect, which resulted in his apprehension materializing, and he did not get the job.

Kelly applied for the same position but approached the issue differently. She was sure she would get the job. She also visualized herself, making a decent perception and taking the job during the week before the interview. She packed her clothes she was going to wear and slept a little earlier in the evening before the interview. The day of the interview, she woke up earlier than usual and had plenty of time to eat breakfast and to arrive before the scheduled time for the interview. Since she made a good impression, she got the job. Of course, she also had the right qualifications for the job, but so did Ashley.

From these two stories, what do we learn? There's some magic involved. No, everything is normal. When the action is good, we have nice feelings and optimistic thoughts and see what we really want to do in our minds. It gives the eyes luminosity, vitality, and joy. The whole being transmits goodwill, happiness, and success. Even education is beneficially affected. We go high, and the voice becomes louder. Our body language shows how you feel inside.

We are both infectious, whether it be Positive Thinking or Negative Thinking.

All of us affect the people we encounter in one-way or another. It occurs naturally and subconsciously, by the movement of thoughts and feelings and the language of the body. People feel our aura and our emotions are influenced, and vice versa. Is it any wonder we would like to be around positive people and avoid negative people?

People are more willing to support us if we are optimistic, and they despise anyone who expresses negativity and rejects it.

Negative thoughts, expressions, and behaviors create negative moods and depressed behavior. If the mind of an individual is pessimistic, it creates more dissatisfaction and negativity. This is the road to disappointment, anger, and deceit. What are the main causes of negative attitudes?

Negative attitudes arise from both the thinking of negative emotions over and over until they are a part of your unconscious-a part of your personality. You may not even know that you have a negative attitude because it was so long with you. You predict failure and catastrophe once you have a bad attitude. This perception makes you a potent magnet for disaster and failure. Then it turns into a vicious circle. You predict the worst—you get the worsty—our confidence is reinforced—you expect the worst—you get the worst. Do you get the picture?

HOW CAN WE CREATE A POSITIVE ATTITUDE AND SHIFT OUR THOUGHTS?

It takes work, but it takes work to create something of quality. We need to shift our unconscious mind-set to have a new attitude. How are we going to do this? Through evaluating every thought, we have until it becomes a habit of positive thinking. You simply swap an old habit with a healthy habit, just like substituting cigarette dependence. You can't just stop being pessimistic, replacing negative thoughts with positive thoughts.

Many people would say, "But bad things are a reality, only happening in everyday life." That's not true at all. Situations, indeed, are a fact. They show up, but it's your ATTITUDE that makes a positive or negative situation. It's time for you to understand how you decide what you think and feel—nobody else on earth has that power unless you give it away. Take control of your mind-set and take control of your outcomes.

"The state of mind establishes the state of your performance."

To turn the mind towards the positive, it takes inner work and training. There is no change in attitude or feelings overnight.

Hold at least a copy of Norman Vincent Peale's Positive Thinking or all of his books on this subject. Read them, understand the important points, think about the advantages, and encourage yourself to try them out. The power of thoughts is a powerful force that influences our life all the time. Typically, this shaping is performed subconsciously, but the mechanism can be made conscious. Even if the idea seems strange, try it, as you have nothing to lose, but only to make a profit. Ignore what others might say or think of you if they notice you're changing your way of thinking.

Visualize conditions that are only desirable and helpful. Use positive words when talking to others in your inner dialogues. Smiling more, as a result, is positive. Neglect any feelings of laziness or willingness to quit. When you persevere, the way your mind thinks and the way you live your life, it will be changed.

When your mind is invaded by a negative thought, you must be mindful of it and, instead, try to replace it with a positive one. Negative thinking will begin to get into your mind again, and then you need to replace it with a constructive one again. It's like two pictures are in front of you, and you choose to look at one of them and ignore the other. Persistence will gradually teach the mind positive thinking and ignore negative thinking.

When you feel some internal resistance while exchanging negative thoughts with positive ones, do not give up, just keep looking in your mind only to the helpful, better, and happy thoughts.

It doesn't matter what your current circumstances are. Think positively; just expect positive outcomes and conditions, and circumstances will change accordingly. The changes may take some time, but eventually, they do.

Some Techniques for Positive Thinking

Why do you always want something to improve your life? Have you ever thought something might be missing, but you did not know what? Have you set and fallen short of targets? You likely, like many of us, have sunk into a depressive state and given up any hope to improve your life. The field of self-amelioration is vast, and many things have to be learned. Yet these are the first steps that give our lives the most support and the most improvement. It is, therefore, important to start with a technique that gives you the best base from which to work and is easy to master. If someone gave you such a program, would you obey or give it up?

The influence of positive thinking is widely known but often overlooked. Depressed people seem to see the world much more objectively than they look at the moment. The optimist has no rational point of view. Where the gloomy looks are at their pessimistic point of view for 'now' and extend it into the future. A depressive produces an uncompromising view of the future in which it makes reasonable demands and assumes a great deal of deceit. Like a prophecy that fulfils itself, they are usually correct.

The optimist, using positive thinking methods, sees the potential in everything. He builds an enticing future that motivates him. He gives himself straightforward, optimistic objectives and wishes to motivate his actions. He has the problems of what the distressed call 'unrealistic expectations.' This key factor in true happiness, allows the optimist to pursue his objectives further. When he is beaten, he knows to try again, but be more 'imaginative'. The optimist, inspired by his imagination, constructs his own vision.

As we can see, a valuable tool that can be used to transform lives and make dreams a reality is the power of positive thinking. Nonetheless, as with many issues, there are very few clear sources of practical information on how positive thinking can be practiced down to earth. I'm certain that you don't want to be without the benefits, and you've definitely had some ambiguous, imprecise suggestions that you've quickly abandoned. For those who think that they can stick to at least one year's four fundamental principles, they are amazed at the changes that such simple techniques bring. I am now presenting you with the four fundamental principles of positive thinking: 1) You are not your man.

You're not your character. You likely were more unique as a kid than you are today as an adult. Yes, a kernel of resemblance will exist, but much of what you do daily, although you might call it this, is not your personality. Your so-called personality is instead, a set of behaviors developed from interactions as a defined mechanism for managing everyday life. Your imaginary character will hold you in life because it determines what you are going to do and what you are unable to do. A woman might feel that she can't be an effective public speaker because she is shy all her life. It actually doesn't happen, and she just needs to learn what makes a good public speaker and follow such mannerisms herself.

You should not accept the idea that whichever age you are at; you are not able to be truly effective in positive thinking. You could be whatever you want to be. In other words, we want to do things that seem unlike what we feel comfortable with. We tell ourselves we can't go skydiving or something like that. These opposing wishes are so important. You should take them and make them come true. These are the way your mind seeks to increase your exposure to new ideas, to escape from the prison that you call personality.

Pick one thing today that you never did but were always curious about. Make a list of months of things you may not be able to do. Run a marathon, join the local drama club and spend a day outside without checking in. You will be astounded by how motivated you feel – and it will inspire you to push back your so-called identity.

2) Learn how to get inspired.

Many of us think we're at the mercy of the day. On a good day, we will do well, and on a bad day, we'll be unmotivated and do little. You have to accept the idea that your day is yours, that you are only at a time where you are willing to respond to the circumstances. Planning ahead will ensure the safety of the so-called unexpected contingency plans. See if there is a way to solve them effectively for those problems that continue to emerge. Once you have as much minimized a situation as possible, the next greatest field of motivation must be established.

Many of us, particularly those new to self-improvement, are influenced by our emotions. Rather, our inability to control our own feelings. Motivation comes by knowing that we have a mission that challenges us, is not unbeatable, and provides a meaningful outcome. You will help unleash the inspiration inside your daily activities by making sure all your big tasks fall into these categories.

Furthermore, plan the office so that there are no disruptions. Get the air, fresh types, pencils, and paper ready in the vicinity. Make sure that the distractions are as few as possible. Once you've done that, you should focus on improving your own attitude - maybe have a list of your favorite uplifting songs, for example. Have a priority list of your day's tasks and tick them as you progress with them. Written records of your successes are an ideal way to build incomplete trust tasks.

Once you are able to plan and use the power of these activities to empower yourself, you feel much more in charge of your workplace. This extra protection helps build your trust and allows you to see things more positively.

Make a list of activities today and see how your inspiration can be motivated.

3) Be sure who you are becoming.

Often people can put you down, knowingly or unknowingly. It can make you aware of your handwriting, your weight, or your lack of trust. At that moment, these words can hurt and cause deep pain and even ruin your day—can put you through your self-perception and trigger a negative spiral that sabotages any positive thinking. Instead of dwelling on why another person does what they did, I don't want you to be a victim, focus on another thing. Being a victim can never produce a positive result. This embodies feelings of impotence and makes you vulnerable to others' whims. If there is any way, you can stop feelings of victimhood, make positive use of the criticism.

You probably think—easy to say—but what's good about the insult? I believe you should use fuel, fuel to prove the other person wrong—to know that who you are today does not have to be who you are tomorrow, or who you are next week, or who you are next year.

If you are dissatisfied with what you condemn, then determine whether the time is right now for something to be done and to overshadow the critical negative person with your own personal power. Those who often judge love to believe you will always be suffering from any question they perceive or "want to perceive." This tells you and the world that you can change, that you can be whatever you want to be. Don't let other people or you define yourself as a static, unchanging being, always burdened by the same distresses.

4) Create the future – dedicate yourself

Suppose it's now been a month. You worked on the three ideas above, and you are beginning to see results. Now that you've learned to solve your own issues, you can inspire and move your own limits – it's time to create your own future. A life so far from where you were, a month ago, or even now, that it would have been impossible to imagine before. Perhaps you want to be a model, lose weight, or increase your income dramatically. Perhaps you want to go to the stage of a popular theatre or start a career as a performer. Look into the future to 20 years and determine where you want to be, regardless of viability or indignation.

Now take the facts and visualize a scene in your mind that illustrates them all. Picture your future self, radiant, and smiling in the picture. Now through the picture lighten the color, smile and bring your thumb and forefinger together. Do this technique of visualization as many times as you recall every day. Press your thumb and finger together as you smile and picture yourself coming to life in the picture. This helps us tie the vision for the future to physical action. Whenever you feel insecure or unmotivated, press your thumb and forefinger together, and you'll have an amazing increase in energy and happiness.

The next step is to prepare how you can achieve your goals in the months, weeks, and years ahead. Take a look at your target and then step back and add key points that will drive your progress. This stage must include sub-goals that help to achieve the main goal.

Chapter 5:
When Does Positive Thinking Become Dangerous?

We are programmed to look for satisfaction and avoid pain. It is so deeply rooted in our unconscious that it motivates all of us. There has recently been a trend towards positive thinking as a way to overcome our obstacles and dissipate negative emotions.

Yet despite the hundreds of millions of dollars spent on retreats, seminars, books, and self-help DVDs on how to positively banish the pain by talking, bad things continue to happen. Wives and husbands are lying, jobs are being lost, disasters are taking place, diseases are emerging, and life is a mixture of good days and bad days.

It may be necessary to step back and realize what a negative experience actually means by the constant drive to feel everything is good. For several people, the issues they face are a great opportunity to learn and develop as they reflect. Through adversity, we learn our most precious life lessons, and this is how we grow.

Negative experiences or perceptions, which at that time are considered to be negative, can also cause a complete shift in our worldview or thought. Spiritual development often follows tragedies, traumatic events, and experiences that change a life. Therefore, the person who works in difficulties may discover new skills, internal strengths, and abilities and not realize what they possessed. Do you recall being resourceful, positive, and totally focused on the issue right now? We are at our best when we are questioned. If we are in a situation, we figure out who we are.

Why are we so frustrated with all this positive thinking?

The disadvantage of the technique may, in fact, be understanding how positive thinking leads to every question in life. If you assume you should think away all the bad issues, how do you justify these things that are not good in your life? You ask yourself whether you are perhaps not as effective with positive thinking learning as you should be. Do you feel like a failing person?

Many people who follow the positive thought teachings and self-help programs will find that the results are an increased sense of failure and depression if the program is not effective. After all, the newest self-help guru is busy telling you how your life will always be fantastic if you follow his or her simple formula. If we do not achieve the degree of satisfaction, our failure must be. Add to that the society's constant messages about what we should wear, weigh, eat, want, and dream, and you have the perfect formula for depression and despondency. With the growing number of people taking medicines for depression, the results of this kind of thinking are all too obvious.

Is There a Better Way?

Rather than looking for someone or something outside of ourselves to make us happy, many of the ancient texts and scriptures encourage us to look inside for our own personal meaning and happiness. The first step in the path to improving and embracing ourselves for who we really are is to learn how to listen to our own internal guidance and purpose.

Working out why we take the negative behaviors that form our day is also an important part of our personal development. Some of the habits can be learned from infancy. These can include harassment, negative behavior, the sharing of rumors and gossip, and our relationships with others. Certain characteristics may include self-criticism, self-harm, or dependence. If we can see them for what they are and begin to make changes in the way we view others, and ourselves, we can lose the pain. This can be very challenging, and since these behaviors mask deeper pain, however, you will be on a very rewarding path if you begin to look into the past and work through it. It requires great personal strength and awareness, and this phase alone really allows us to make the changes that will give us a desperate peace and happiness.

It takes time to accept yourself and to learn to love others, especially if you have experienced pain, rejection, or animosity in your own life. This certainly cannot be done on a weekend retreat or by taking a class. This kind of work takes a lifetime, but progress should be seen relatively quickly. It is vital to be surrounded by good, happy people who will help and guide you as you find your way.

For some, this path to transformation and personal growth makes more sense than depending solely on the power of positive thinking. While some people use positive thinking with great results, they are usually not the ones with deeper problems. Positive thinking has its place; after all, it's much more pleasant to look for the positive and be around those who are optimistic, than to hang around a pessimist.

Many people have positive thinking plans for disappointment. It refers to those people who have to change their way of life to make the changes they are looking for. People who need medications and qualified assistance will not thrive only by thinking more positively. People who are addicted to drugs, alcohol, obsessive-compulsive behavior, and unhealthy habits like cigarettes or overeating cannot just stop thinking about their own problems. Like everyone else, these people should start by looking at why they do what they do before any actual, permanent change can take place.

While positive thinking will enable you to reach a certain degree of satisfaction, it is often not a true long-term improvement. For most people, the better option is to live every moment and embrace it as it is. This means you can be sad, happy, challenged, or pleased, whatever happens in reality. You must not forget what is happening in times of adversity or struggle. Some of the lessons of life are to be learned by going through the bad spot so that when they arrive, you enjoy the happy times. Determine your own strengths and abilities to react honestly and objectively to all of the issues in your life.

Staying positive and motivated is a good idea, but it allows us to grow and develop internally and spiritually so that real feelings are exposed and felt. Bear in mind that when life changes, things get better, and the sun is always waiting for the opportunity to shine again behind every cloud. Rejoice and learn from times of suffering and struggle in moments of joy. Times of struggle are times of growth, plus the environment in which you live in a safe, natural way to live.

Transform Your Life Through Your Habits

Roses are blue, violets are orange, but bad habits are as relaxing as cozy beds. They're really simple to get into but very hard to get out of. So, I'll ask you, look at your feelings, because they're usually words. Watch your words because they become deeds. Control your acts because they become patterns.

Look at your patterns because they're becoming characters. Look at your story, and it will be your destiny. Not your real destiny, but your own. Bad habits can disrupt the representation of our destiny. In fact, due to their bad habits, many people have gone to their grave with unfulfilled potential. And our bad habits go, as we can see.

The question is basically about unconscious patterns. We tend to continue to do what we are used to, rather than choosing our best option. Yet, rather than changing our patterns, we are more likely to repeat the pattern whenever we want because of the control power of bad habits. But be assured, you will learn today three simple steps that will help you manage all the behaviors, instead of controlling them. They call these simple steps: cause, creation, and transformation.

Here's the first simple step we should think about: Cause, the importance of cause is what caused something to happen. What I mean is, cause is the root cause of a habit. Usually, there is no smoke without a spark. Cause detects trends that cause behavior. For example, the organization in which the habit usually happens, what kind of thoughts the habit causes, and how often the habit happens every day. This will enable us to get used to it.

After that, once popular, Dr. Phil says we can't fix what we can't recognize. We all have bad habits; let's face it. To help us stop, tell yourself what your habits cost you. Since habits are robbers, among other things, they can steal your time, your happiness, or your confidence. A habit of negative self-talk, for example, can steal trust, a habit of unhealthy eating can steal a positive self-image, and a habit of laziness can rob future success.

You did not form your customs in one day in the same way; so don't expect to avoid them in one day. It will take some time, effort, and consistency. You know, though, that you're worth it. Recognize that you have a problem and begin to work on it today. Making a habit is not always free, but maintaining your habits can cost you more. It will cost you your happiness, well being, and independence.

So, I'll talk about the second simple step: transformation.

Transformation is the improved version of you, but you have to adjust first before you transform yourself. Any change in life is only temporary, without changing the underlining bad habits first. For example, someone with low self-esteem and a cosmetic operation to feel better about himself will only feel better for a short time before he discovers something else he wants to change because he is trying to solve an internal problem with external interventions, such as poor self-esteem. Without changing the habitual pattern that led to a problem, it is only temporary to get rid of low self-esteem.

It is easy to see that when you want to change something in your life, you start to change the underlying habit. This means that we can't continue to do the same thing and expect another outcome. 1 + 1 is always going to be 2. If we do the same thing, then we're still going to get the same result. The good news is, however, that research shows that it takes just 21 days to create a new habit, so start today.

On the other side, what is considered stimuli typically activate our behaviors. In reality, you do not respond to lives in the way you do, but rather your causes and conditioning. Children going to school, for instance, can be led to hunger by the school bell, which is not surprising. The fact is, if you hear the lunch bell, whether you are hungry or not, you are hungry immediately. But, if the bell that is the trigger can be avoided, let us say on school holidays, they avoid the emotional hunger created by the bell, after approximately 21 days of the new habit.

In the same way, it will help us to recognize, prevent, and replace psychological stimuli. This is referred to as positive feedback. With that being said, if it's your cup of tea, negative feedback can motivate you to kick your habits. Negative feedback involves putting a rubber tape on your wrist, so you snap the rubber band to your wrist whenever you are tempted. Ouch, she knows what she likes. Honestly, however, negative feedback shapes the mind to overcome the habit of ignoring pain. Nevertheless, both positive and negative feedback works. And you have the option.

The third simple step I'll talk about is learning.

The formation is something forming an act. But by creation, she means the formation of new good habits, the removal of the bad ones, to change your life.

Consider something else to divert you from your practice. The devil's hands are idle. And typically, our emphasis is our desire. Find something positive that overlooks your habits, your desires. For example, someone who has a pessimistic way of thinking and wants to starve to death by positive self-talking. This person is going to starve to death and then develop a new positive attitude.

In addition, find a new hobby to improve your strengths or a new hobby to help you develop new strengths. For example, learn to play music, learn to write, or to paint is a great way of avoiding bad habits. These are also therapeutic activities. Be wary of what she called the condition of the comfort zone. Since every time you move out from a familiar place, that is your comfort zone, because of the fear of the unknown, you will develop some anxieties. All you have to do is hold yourself out of fear. Continue to consider what you have to gain from breaking your habit. If you are consistent for about 21 days, you lose the fear of staying away from unwelcome habits and instead gain more confidence.

Finally, as famously said by Shaquille O'Neal, "you are where you are frequently." And she says to you, "rather than what you want, make a habit of just doing things that you want."

How to Live a Healthy Life with Good Habits

A healthy wellbeing, and wellness, without a doubt, is our greatest desire. After all, life dramatically changes its meaning without health. In the future, the only way to feel happy, energetic, and safe is to live a happy, energetic, and healthy life. The advantages and pleasures are immediate and long-term.

We walk even more in a direction where people finally know that being safe is not just sick.

We cannot permit life to pass on through without living it with stimuli and energy that communicate our happiness. By simply taking a strong, constructive, and participatory approach towards them, we will make our lives more desirable and relaxing.

We can't stop the path of life many times. Nevertheless, life is also the product of our attitudes and actions. So, we are the product of our experiences.

What is a healthy life?

"What needs to happen in order to be healthy?" are questions people often ask themselves, "how do I begin a healthy life" and "how do I achieve a healthy and happy life."

Firstly, Debrucemo: what does it even mean to be healthy? Health is the 'mental, social, and physical wellbeing rather than the mere absence of sickness,' according to the World Health Organization (WHO). In other words, being healthy is simply the physical and mental wellbeing of the patient, not only the absence of diseases. It is no coincidence that the WHO thus describes health and gives the term a much broader meaning than the mere antonyms of disease.

While health clearly tends to be synonymous with the word medicine, this goes far beyond the meaning that common sense frequently refers to, usually only associating it with curative medicine. Nevertheless, medicine is much more than that because it is mainly concerned with disease prevention.

Lifestyles, poor diet, stress, etc., also led to the aggravation of problems. Types include obesity and high blood pressure, conditions that are closely linked to modern peoples' behaviors.

Many of the problems of modern medicine can be easily avoided by following some of the main recommendations for a healthy lifestyle.

It is imperative and urgent to change habits and behaviors. That doesn't mean that we should obey all the rules for a healthy life in the text, as though it were a complicated, painful, even castrating plan. Life has to be lived with passion and pleasure, so we must never be mere prisoners of our attitudes or habits that are both painful and restricting, while healthier.

Life consists of choices. Get educated, seek a balance between the advantages and disadvantages of your personal tastes, towards a healthier life, and note that you want to improve your quality of life eventually.

We speak about changing attitudes that inspire us and make us happy, thus improving our wellbeing. It is not always possible, it is real, but it is perfectly feasible in the vast majority of cases.

Think of a simple walk in the wild and enjoy your favorite fruit, for example. These are two simple examples of how you can enjoy life and improve your health simultaneously.

Healthy living is also in our possession through water and physical exercise. Don't think that we can eat excessive amounts of sugar daily and that if we end up suffering from diabetes one day, it is simply a matter of destiny and misfortune. They cannot judge those who are depressed at high doses each day and will not pay a high price for it continuously. Let us not say that we have been smokers for years and let us not lift breathing difficulties and degrade our quality of life.

Our attitudes make us think about our wellbeing sooner or later.

The attitude toward life is clearly a decisive factor in making it safer. Think of life as optimistic and feel good before any practice.

There are two important things to remember. Firstly, nutrition, a good diet can do much more than you know about your health. The definition of food and healthy living is indissoluble.

Secondly, prepare a fitness regime. When this is done in the right way, your health and wellbeing can significantly improve, thus contributing to a better quality of life.

Think of physical exercise as optimistic and calming, not as unpleasant, and "something that must be done." Figure out what event you like the most and see the advantages it can offer.

Adjust these two factors, and live a healthier life.

Get quality of life. How many of us still experience the discomfort of simple back pain? Perhaps you felt the pain caused by repeated illnesses, often because our immune system was weakened.

Nevertheless, we all know from many studies that illness and pain dramatically decrease our quality of life.

We live today in an age when it is time to set laws. The lack of time drives people to live against this precious commodity in a constant race.

We have no time to eat healthily, and we have no time for physical exercise, we have no time to speak to others, we have no time for many things that are important to our lives. Unfortunately, such habits produce a variety of problems with serious health and wellbeing implications.

On the one hand, people are strongly impacted by these issues, and on the other, their quality of life is severely degraded.

In short, they would say that a good quality of life is not possible without healthy habits.

Get Healthy and longevity. Average life expectancy was significantly lower a couple of decades ago.

It gradually increased with improvements in conditions of life and progress in medicine. It's still because we all want to live longer and better.

The current objective is not only to live longer. It must have a sustainable lifestyle, that is, an active, safe, happy and purpose-focused life. Yet living longer doesn't mean living better. The increase in life expectancy also comes at the expense of more or less advanced therapies that, while successful, seriously damage the quality of life of people. Not only should we want to live more, but we should also live better.

Longevity is in our possession, as well. They evasively assume that we must focus our attention on maintaining a healthy lifestyle, believing that our present behaviors will have an important impact on our future health.

If you want to live better and longer, then begin to take steps in this direction that are positive, balanced, and contribute to your overall wellbeing.

Obtain Healthy life results.

The benefits of healthy living for people are innumerable. Therefore, it is not necessary to describe them with the extractor because we all know how good it is to be well, or rather to feel sick.

However, there are no ends to the benefits of healthy living. Healthcare costs are becoming increasingly disadvantageous, either directly or indirectly, by way of public health taxes.

There are findings that clearly show that we can make significant savings with curative medical therapies for every dollar invested in prevention.

In other words, expenditure focus should be geared towards disease prevention. On the other hand, the social and economic costs caused by disease, such as work absenteeism, are very substantial with rising social protection expenses.

Health & Wellness. There is an overwhelming interest in curative health today, in which medicine has grown, in recent years, exponentially. As we saw, these advances in medicine have unquestionably resulted in people living a longer and better quality of life.

In the absence of nutrition, our entire life is diminished, and therefore, we cannot live and enjoy it entirely.

Therefore, we need to focus on our future because the way we live now also represents our quality of life.

A new paradigm needs to evolve in order to promote wellness and strong attitudes of individuals towards disease prevention, with tremendous health benefits, enhancement of their quality of life and wellbeing. In short, we all want to build a healthier lifestyle in which health comes first.

For all these purposes, we evasively conclude that the dedication to disease prevention, health, and welfare promotion is of the utmost importance.

Chapter 6:
Refection of Bad Habits

These are some of the strategies that I have discovered that seem to motivate me to improve some of my less than admirable habits.

Start Slow Lose Focus Wear a Record One at a time when you are accountable. This is how every method works: Start small modifying a trend can't involve an attitude of everything or nothing.

Practice Instance: Cutting off the daily stream of soft drinks might start by restricting one in the morning and one in the evening, ensuring that you have plenty of water between them. Then you can slowly work down to one in the morning and remain strong until you have completely cut them off.

The Switch: Coffee offers numerous health benefits; as countless studies have confirmed. Exercise to substitute soft drinks with a coffee in the morning will not only provide you with an effective start to the day but may also help reduce your risk of type 2 diabetes, cancers, or even strokes.

Avoid triggers: Both candy and sweetened drinks have been scientifically proven to trigger people's appetite for soft drinks. Drinking water and snacks should, therefore, be the end goal for somebody who struggles with this problem.

Other uses: The work-to-down approach is also suitable for snacking, cigarettes, consuming food, drinking, and shopping.

Lose Focus: If you find yourself in an unhealthy pattern, change the atmosphere immediately.

Example: If you go into the kitchen to grab a snack, you don't need to turn around instantly and do something else, anything else.

Switch: Switch your concentration with something as simple as fluffing pillows on the sofa, open blinds all over the house, plug in a laundry wash or check your email or text messages. Get out of the kitchen.

Avoidable trigger: If you are used to snacking every day at a certain time, adjust your routine, so you do an activity that doesn't involve you near the food at that time.

Other use: The loss of focus on behavior could also work for people with warm temperatures, online gambling trends, excessive TV viewing habits, and social media obsessions.

Wear a reminder: Once an inappropriate behavior has been detected, keep track of it.

Exemplary practice: When you know that your teen's constant argument and speech will get a glimpse of you, wear a big, sexy, cheap finger-ring (something you don't need to feel and see) that will be a constant reminder of what is necessary when you try to deal with issues constructively.

The Switch: Rather than looking at a ring and saying, "stay calm," which sadly would brace you for the unfortunate situation that could never happen, look into the ring and say, "I love this child really and am glad about the person they are learning to become." For example, I have created a homework log that has helped our family with school-related issues.

Some Use: It is fairly easy to train yourself to associate an unknown thing psychologically with your unwanted behavior. Certain examples of bad behavior, which can be influenced easily by this process, include pacing when driving, biting your fingernails, forgetting a daily task, spending too much time on the phone and never seeming to have been dressed up for the day. Nothing like a piece of flashy jewelry reminding you that you're in holey shorts!

One at a time, it is not only difficult to switch an entire lifestyle at once, but it leads to a certain disappointment. Put all your time and energy into modifying a rule before you regulate it, and then take your next goal.

Practice Example: Although most people feel they are married fairly well, difficulties sometimes occur because of a lack of effective communication. Make your mind to close this void.

The Switch: Instead of constantly using the same failing methods to open up communication channels and hoping for a different result, seek to abandon any past approaches that have not succeeded and replaced them in the future with new, action-orientated ideas.

An example of a tactic is that both parties can vigorously speak about issues and heatedly debate different points of view. Most often, no partner reacts favorably to this strategy, but people continue to use it.

Another tactic to try is to only make a simple but sincere declaration of what you need and move forward with each other—the start of the argument.

Trigger to avoid respecting that certain issues may need to be discussed in more detail but understanding that there is probably a better time and place, set time for tackling the problem in the near future (later on the day or during the week). At that time, it could have fixed itself, or at least you both had time to think critically about options before coming together.

Other uses: It is best to try to change only one pattern at a time, and in most situations, it should succeed. Too thin does not only frustrate yourself but everyone around you who does not understand the abrupt change of personality and lifestyle.

Responsible - Once, you have decided to change your behavior let someone around you know your personal search and ask them to help keep you on track.

Practice Example: It's a challenge for many people to spend physically inactive, either because of school, endless home duties, or just idle play. Once you've made up your mind, hire a good friend or close family member to help.

The Switch: Create a standing "appointment" with your trustee, instead of depending on an opening on your calendar to allow you to have fast practice. This may be every night or day, but it needs to be logical, practical, and easy to reach. You might even consider talking on the phone while practicing "together."

Avoidable trigger: realize that helping your trustee is not a choice. Schedule a time that is really workable and negotiate backup plans early in case you can't meet extremes. Just stand up and do it. Being sleepy, cold, in a bad mood, we don't have many other reasons to come up with.

Certain Uses: This technique must be used. You are ashamed about the actions you want to improve, but, once you 'announce', that you don't like anything about yourself, you won't only draw attention to that possible weakness, but you will look weak or like a 'flake' if you don't succeed. Perhaps the more people you tell, the better.

The Secret of Building Mental Resilience

During difficult economic times, it can be increasingly difficult to maintain a positive attitude. Nonetheless, keep in mind that the same strategies and life skills will work regardless of the circumstances. We human beings are created to solve problems, and we are supposed to be happy!

It can be frustrating and stressful if a woman loses her job, fails a test, or fails with a loved one. Will you know what to do? If life brings you a bunch of limes, do you fall apart and try to recover for months, or are you resilient? Do you get better with the ups and downs and hide under a rock until the storm blows? It is particularly important to be flexible and prepared for anything during these difficult times.

Resilient people become more "mentally tough." Think of them like Energizer Bunnies, they go and go. But how can you grow power and perseverance of this kind? What is their identity, what is their secret?

Resilience is a feature that many people have. Those who are resilient will surmount difficult situations and stay cool, calm, and collected. You are ready to look for options and follow suit. You can't deter disappointments from what you want. Rather, they remain focused and plan to succeed. We can all learn to be stronger and better mentally. It's all about being better mentally, physically, and emotionally to perform at the highest level. Success is how we work, act, breathe, think, do our job. Wherever we conduct these roles and duties, it is important to know how well we do it and how we can enhance or modify it. Ask yourself in which state you are.

How do you do all these things? Were you happy? Are you happy? Are you happy with life as it is now?

If you want more from your life, whether to do well in your job, be promoted to the next level, or spend more time with your family and friends, then it's time to start working at the highest levels.

There are seven strategies here to help you become more resilient and mentally tough: 1) Start breathing. This exercise prepares the body for improved performance. Right now, are you holding your breath? If you are stressed or anxious, you may not just breathe, but you may have headaches, backaches, and straining shoulders. This is a treatment for you: Take three deep breaths and slowly let them out. Count one, two, and three. Count one, two. It creates good circulation and steady breathing throughout the remainder of the day.

2) Get more exercise. You name it. Anything that pumps your heart causes significant body changes. A woman has a sense of control, and as we all know, control, as humans, is important to us! Fitness practices such as

running, walking, yoga and Pilates, cycling, hiking, swimming, or any sport, are all good ways to keep the mind and body safe.

3) Give the energy your body needs. Food fuels the human motor. When you're about to go on a long drive, you won't go home without putting gas in your car, but you might not think about leaving for work twice without having breakfast. Where is the meaning? Fill your tank with energizing whole yogurt, vegetables, grains, and see your quality grow.

4) Have a laugh. When it gets hard, the hard one starts to laugh! Go out and find your fun. Whether it's a comedy club, a funny movie, or a special comedy mate, now is the time to find your funny bone and to increase your feel-good endorphins. This not only helps with your emotional state but also with your physical being. Think about it. You breathe while you smile. Do it, chuckle a big bowl, and see what's going on. Have you noticed how much better you feel after a funny movie?

5) The vision of your future. Practice what you want and see clearly for your life what you want. It may seem crazy, but it can open new possibilities, whether it's an ability you're trying to achieve or a dream house you

want to move into. Athletes always do it. You will see the ball entering the hole or the basketball entering the net. Think, and it will be: "This achievement is mine." The bottom line is that mentally tough people use their brains. It has to be done. Now, go out and play brain games. Try the right-brain-left-brain drills, including puzzles, cards, and memory games. Brush your hair (or teeth) with the opposite hand. Figure out a way to get home after work. We use only 11% of our brainpower, which means 89% of our brain is waiting to get used to it. Speak about all this possibility!

7) Be cool. Be cool. Mentally tough people know how to stay calm and suppress feelings. Here are some tips: try a bit of biofeedback; spend the afternoon dreaming; listen to music; have a happy dog. Ultimately, but not least, get rid of the negative ideas! For example, quit "I can't," and substitute it with, "I can or I will." Especially women who choose to be positive, resilient, and mentally difficult! Happiness is a mental state, not a location, an item, an individual, or an object. Consider the rules of appeal. You're attracting what you believe. Mentally tough people are happy and know that it is up to them to do so. You do know that training makes it really great. The good news is that all this costs nothing at all. You

don't have to go and buy a handbook or just a single piece of costly equipment.

Times are hard...but we can get strong and learn a lot from them. Be comfortable and psychologically strong, and you can handle whatever is in your way!

What is Mental Toughness

This is one of the many reasons why it is important for children to participate in balanced extra-curricular activities organized at a young age: gymnastics, karate, music, ballet, children and youth in the church, scouts, or youth sport will play a part in initiating the discipline and structure necessary to be mentally developed. Note that I said I started playing a part. This takes time to plan.

Developing mental strength, (and leadership skills), is also a reason to allow athletes to engage in an adequate training program at the age of 14 or 15. A training program helps not only to build strength, stamina but also to improve mentally. Any mentor (trainer, manager, etc.), as well as the camaraderie and support of a small group, should be accountable for the players, even though it is only one or two people.

If the player participates in a training program before 14 or 15, they should be for agility and speed training and teach the proper techniques in weightless strength conditioning. Please consult your child's doctor during their annual physical examination before beginning any training program, because all children's development is different.

Defining mental toughness has the psychological edge that helps one to perform at a peak level of effort and performance during training, practice, or competition requirements. In general, when the demands are higher or, the circumstances are adverse.
Whenever the demands are highest, the cognitive toughness characteristics are most apparent.
Some of the numerous features evident when a player is psychically hard can include: self-confidence, self-motivation, focus, concentration, calmness, self-control, positive energy, determination, persistence, leading. This doesn't mean that the result is always the winner; these

characteristics can most frequently appear in the event of a loss. But over time, the mental strength of skilled players is evident in winning championships, with diligent preparation.

To become mentally resilient, one must practice qualities leading to mental toughness. I want a rule to follow, but it doesn't. It takes time and patience to develop mental strength under the right leadership. Parents, teachers, coaches, and other mentors should be active in the training process regularly.

Failure and the ability to bounce back also take place. Most people develop mental strength through failure. Good parents don't want to disappoint their children, and I understand that. Still, though, far too many blame others for their failure. Parents easily blame teachers for class problems or a coach when the child is not excellent at an event. Mental toughness cannot be developed properly when others are blamed. In truth, the reverse is true.

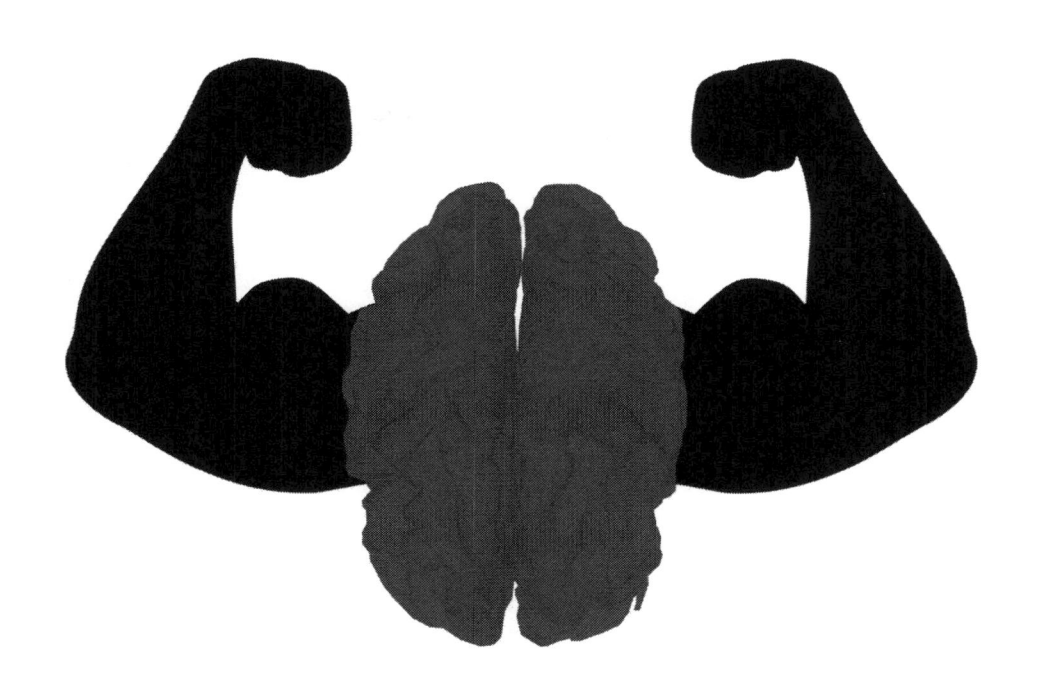

Chapter 7:
Mental Toughness—High Frustration Tolerance

Would we change who we are, what we feel, and also how we behave? Can a leopard change its spots? I recently talked to somebody who asked if a psychologist is just painting over the spots of the "leopard," and underneath, we all stay the same. Okay, I don't see many leopards in my consultation room, but I see people still shifting. A positively changed mind-set is important for cognitive strength and resilience. Read on, and I will continue to discuss this issue.

The fundamental difference between a leopard, a dog, a tree, and a human being is that other living things have already figured out their course and purpose. A leopard will become a leopard; a tree will do what a leopard does. The manual for directions is included.

It is our duty to us human beings, who and what we are in every moment. We are self-conscious and self-determined. We are dropped into the world with no script or stage directions as actors on a stage. We don't have a manual of instructions. That is why our responsibility is who we are and what we become. Of course, there are factors that affect who we are today and which I have mentioned below, but the important point I am trying to make in this regard is that these factors cannot be overused as excuses for our future. It is our duty to us human beings, who and what we are in every moment. We are self-conscious and self-determined. We are dropped into the world with no script or stage directions as actors on a stage. We don't have a manual of instructions. That is why our responsibility is who we are and what we become. Of course, there are factors that affect who we are today and which I have mentioned below, but the important point I am trying to make in this regard is that these factors cannot be overused as excuses for our future.

Family and culture: What we are could be said to be the product of our education and community. We may have accepted messages and information from other people and the world about ourselves. For example, because we are "lazy," "no good," "good for nothing," or "not expected to succeed," we may have accepted ideas about others that are unintelligent or barbarous, mean, and controlled. We may think that the world is typically dangerous, carefree, or unfriendly. The fact is these ideas could have been kept alive and continued to be accepted uncritically and not reassessed. If we did, then this is our decision, and we must continue to believe it.

DNA and genetics in terms of our DNA and genetics, we have little selection. 50% of our parents and 25% of each grandparent are the heritage. We may be more open to some sports and activities, although we will only do that if we have the right tuition and mentoring. We can also inherit physical and mental illness predispositions. Our genes may have an impact, but we are not dogs and racehorses in pedigree shows, we are self-aware freethinking people, and still, determine what our future is at every time.

You are pushed through the atmosphere. Sometimes, it is implied that we are already a reflection of our society and that you will improve the individual when you change the environment. Consider these examples: when you stop homelessness, you can stop crime because when people are poor, they commit a crime. It will be rehabilitated when you punish a thief and praise him for positive actions. The oppressed are "no choice," but terrorists. Teach a young man to play table tennis, and he will give up the sale of drugs and knife his opponents. I think you will agree that life is not that easy, and in their world, people still have choices.

We are driven by inner drives. Are we only at the mercy of our internal drives like drives for fun, energy, and meaning? We are not always rational, conscious people. In our thoughts and actions, our subconscious drives and desires for enjoyment, heat, comfort, physical contact, and gender control. The new field of evolutionary psychology, which explores our actions from the advantages of our ancestors, argues that many of our unconsciousness drives aim at gaining an evolutionary benefit and transmitting our genes. So, we are driven by evolution as well. We are also motivated by our need for influence and our attempts to be superior. For one field, we can compensate for our shortcomings by mastering another and being guided by subconscious objectives. For example, if we are unsuited to sports, we can excel in music. We can also strive to find meaning in conscious life goals and things like work and family. We still have control and responsibility for our lives by understanding these drives and instincts.

And after all of the above, should we change our free will?

I believe you know my answer. When we accept that we are the result of our creation, culture, genetics, the environment, psychology, and evolution, we are only the victims of external influences and internal conditions. As people, we have the right to stand and change beyond our climate and circumstances at all times.

A leopard can't change his spots because he's a leopard, but you can pinch your issues and turn them into goals. Take the idea that the past is all-important; we all have a history, but we must not be the past.

Living a Healthy Life

LONGEVITY: Long-life and great health can be significantly promoted by our nutritional (most important) and physical activities, such as regular exercise.

Regulations and health habits: 1st rule: eat less, and live longer?

Calorie restriction has been one of the strongest measures to control aging, but it is a significant controversy.

Experiments have shown that underfed rodents live 40% longer than their healthy counterparts. The same findings for fruit flies, worms, apes, and other experimental laboratories have been published.

One obvious fact about this is that it's quite a hard task to deal with calories because people who have experienced it will quickly expose themselves to you.

Studies on people who use calorie intake limits found that some ageing predictor, e.g., blood glucose rates, blood pressure, cholesterol, etc. all improved on CR diets.

Because of the challenges facing people trying to limit their calorie intake, the goal is now to find drugs that can give people all the advantages of calorie restriction without diets.

Drugs used to extract the advantages of calorie limitation are not yet approved, but more scientists are interested in this. Work on what occurs at the molecular level when calorie restriction slows down aging, is continuing. These campaigns try to spread information regarding chemicals such as resveratrol, a chemical contained in red wine, and that enhances the length of life of yeast and fruit flies.

The resveratrol, which exists in many forms of life, is released from pressure by the body system. This slows down age when the activity of a molecule called SRT1 is intensified. It explains how the calorie restrictions work, and the body feels a persistent, mild pressure when starving so that it can defend against any more extreme stresses that may cause the cells to get older, i.e., the body cells, to protect themselves from further decay.

If resveratrol could be supplied in the form of tablets, then the body could have succeeded in manipulating itself, believing that it receives not enough calories and then the body's reactions are aimed at defending itself against further deterioration and thus slowing down aging, but this is still an idea that researchers are exclusively interested in now.

Rule 2: Eat right when you look.

People prefer to eat junk food than to eat the right kind of food and thus dig their own early tombs in ignorance.

An average individual presently would have adjusted for the life of fast food joints in the morning, afternoon, and night. Others feel that more expensive cousins add more value to their meat. We do not know that there are many drawbacks to a big rice bowl with a salad dressing plus a big turkey lap etc., that make up a meal for a person when retailed in fast-food joints that could predispose one to illnesses such as diabetes, cancer and many types of heart diseases. Remember some of the issues you might experience.

The intake of a lot of highly processed foods wouldn't satisfy you for a long time and would make you quickly return to more food so that you eat even more than you would need for a day.

Highly prepared food lacks the necessary vitamins to nourish life because many vitamins are water-soluble while others are heat-labile, and so about 80% of the total vitamin contents of the food must have been depleted at a later stage of the processing. Always note that some of these vitamins are called vitamins of fundamental importance because our bodies cannot synthesize them.

Turkey's laps are full of cholesterol, the main cause of atherosclerosis, heart attack, and stroke is high on saturated fat.

The majority of preservatives used in highly processed foods are harmful to the human system (alien). Some are medications that can be converted into harmful metabolites after entering the body, while others have toxic effects when they enter the body.

Most processed foods are colored to make them more attractive to the eyes by adding chemicals. Such additives are typically not licensed by most of the food authorities and should not be used in food preparations.

To avoid these problems mentioned and to achieve a healthy age and longevity, you are advised to always feast on fruit and vegetables.

Which fruit and vegetable products?

Not only are fruits and vegetables good for you, but also they are far too good because they contain several phytochemicals that induce longevity.

What are phytochemicals?

Some are also referred to as supplements. Evidence combined with life evidence indicates that these chemicals help restore good health and quality of life and sustain a long life. We function by removing free radicals that are highly reactive species that are produced by living processes and that cause constant damage to cells and tissues of the body. Sources and their roles of phytochemicals are:

a) Flavonoids; they are naturally grown from citrus fruits, onions, apples, and grapes. A class of phytochemicals is supposed to protect against cancer and other diseases of degeneration. An apple a day for flavonoids helps to prevent cancer. Attach citrus fruit, for example. The oranges and grapes are used to generate variegations and to establish variegations so that you have an interest in your fruit and vegetables and not a monotone apple a day that soon can be of value.

b) Carotenoids make your oranges look orange, give your banana a yellow look, and give your carrots color. They also become vitamin A in your skin. Lutein, zeaxanthin and Lycopene protect against cataracts, against coronary artery diseases, cancer and, against muscle degeneration – all further justification for eating carotenoids.

c) Apples, fiber, grapes, carrots and bananas are considered to be very high in soluble and water - dissolving fiber. This pushes appetite back by limiting digestion and thus helps to reduce calories and ultimately to age. Rich diets with fiber are advised to combat heart disease, diabetes, obesity, cancer, and high blood pressure, all of which contribute to life elongation.

d) Isoflavones, it is understood that certain plant chemicals replicate female natural hormones known to decrease, such as estrogen, in menopausal women. The crop estrogen is a rich source of the isoflavones phytochemical. Use of isoflavones can provide many benefits, such as lower levels of blood lipid, relief from menopausal symptoms, and reduced breast cancer predisposition, ovarian cancer, endometrial cancer, and prostate cancer.

The issue may be with selecting the right amount of vegetables and franchises, likely because many food kinds of literature you've seen and read before sometimes offer conflicting information, so try the following tips.

A glass of juice should be deemed very important every morning. We should also not forget that juice contributes to the calories we eat each day, and we should keep a close eye on our consumption of calories, including the juice we drink. In short, we should remember that not all fruits are similarly advantageous: choose the right vegetables and fruits.

Drink the correct amount to avoid excess calories.

The fruit and vegetable section must include; an apple regularly, - 115 g of blueberries - 115 g of red, green, orange, and yellow - 115 g or a handful of green beans - 185ml of tomato juice.

And typically, between 5-9 portions are recommended in one day. It's a tip.

If you have a lifetime, you must be able to fully change the food you eat and see it as absolutely satisfying.

Eat potatoes, but not too many of them.

CARBOHYDRATE NEED. Potatoes contain no fat, only carbohydrates, which can easily be converted to sugar. In your daily meal, you can include a few potatoes and dress them with other vegetables, not only alone.

Your overall need for carbohydrates should not exceed 60% of your total dietary requirements. Most of the carbohydrates are extracted from grains and cereals. The carbohydrate building blocks or monomeric units are mainly made from fruits and vegetables. Nevertheless, the key carbohydrate is starch, which is the way carbohydrates are processed in plants and primarily derived from cereals and grains.

CEREALS AND GRAINS Rice, corn, bran, while maize and barley are good examples of cereals.

The safest thing for the consumption of cereals and grains is to eat more whole grains than processed for the following reasons,

a) Processed grains and cereals contain less fiber, and are easily digested, and hunger returns faster so that you tend to eat more processed food after.

b) Soluble fiber is more common in whole and unprocessed cereals and grains, which will alleviate hunger by increasing digestion.

Therefore, the recommended total need for carbohydrate can be added to 115 g of whole grain and cereals or the equivalent from processed grain, such as 115 g pasta.

This simple arithmetic gives an answer, 18 calories* your body weight (kg) only, if you weigh 70 kg, you would need about 18 calories* 70(kg)= 1260 cal of carbohydrate every four days.

It is recommended that you should not exceed 18 calories per kg of body weight from carbohydrate sources (fruit, vegetables, cereals, or grains).

Review this table for your recommended daily calories with carbohydrates 18cal / kg 58%-60% 3cal / kg 10%-12% Fats 9cal / kg 30 kg Note; this follow-up continues in the next issue, so keep a record of how to get a good protein and fat requirement that keeps the life of our body long.

2) You will begin to master your diet, and it does not take a lifetime. Just a few days, and you should begin to know various weights of different foods that would keep you healthy.

MEDICAL INFORMATION 80%–90% of diabetes is correlated with a diet and lifestyle.

The avoidance of Type 2 diabetes by avoiding highly refined foods.

Fruits, vegetables, small nutty diary items can reduce high blood pressure.

Secrets of Cultivating a Positive Mind-Set

There are many posts on the Internet that display a positive attitude as wishful thinking and blind optimism. A positive attitude is a key to success. How can one achieve their goals if they are pessimistic and indifferent to life's opportunities? A positive mentality cultivates positive thoughts, leading to positive words and, ultimately, actions. What is a positive attitude? How do you cultivate a positive attitude and maintain it?

What is a positive mind-set?

To understand what a positive attitude is, we need to describe what it isn't; a positive attitude is not blind optimism. Blind optimism is dangerous; it's like being inside your house in a hurricane when waters rise to your eyes, and your house doesn't crash. On the other side, a positive attitude acknowledges the rising floods and believes in recovery and restoration. A positive mind-set, in contrast to cynicism and perceived failure, is based on a learning way of thinking that concentrates on incentives and good results. A positive attitude is cultivated; it is not something given to a chosen birth unit, but rather an achievement. How do you cultivate a positive attitude? To understand what a positive attitude is, we need to describe what it isn't; a positive attitude is not blind optimism. Blind optimism is dangerous; it's like being inside your house in a hurricane when waters rise to your eyes, and your house doesn't crash. On the other side, a positive attitude acknowledges the rising floods and believes in recovery and restoration. A positive mind-set, in contrast to cynicism and perceived failure, is a learning way of thinking that concentrates on incentives and good results. A positive attitude is cultivated; it is not something given to a chosen birth unit, but rather an achievement. How do you cultivate a positive attitude?

There are ten tools to cultivate and maintain a positive attitude.

1. Concentrate on the present How many times have you applied your mind to a problem? How many of these negative results are perceived? When concentrating on the present, you minimize the number of concerns and doubts, leading to negative thinking that can lead to unnecessary action and self-fulfillment.

The next time you find your mind running away from the possible negative consequences, get yourself back to the present. The practice is the secret to concentrating on the present; sadly, nothing else exists. Be vigilant if your mind wonders and note what caused negative thinking. Learn from the past and welcome the present to succeed and to create a life you enjoy.

2. Use positive language; how often do you pay attention to the words you use? Use positive language. How much of what you say is negative? Negative tends to produce more negative effects. Have you ever found that there's never only one thing, but a whole list of things, people, and consequences when people complain?

Our thoughts form our words and thus, create an action. When our thoughts and words are negative, then we will ultimately begin to take action, resulting in a negative result. How are you going to stop this negative cycle?

Willie Nelson said that once you substitute negative thoughts with positive ones, you will get good results. Awareness is the first step to break this negative cycle. Unless you use negative language, change the conversation instantly, and start thinking about things, results, or moments that were a positive experience. Positivity is behavior, and positivity becomes a normal way of being over time.

3. **When I am in a pessimistic state of mind**, it can often be really hard for me to see a positive result or perspective. The easiest way to get out of this negative thought is to ask some open questions.

What can I learn from this?

What is the potential in this situation for me?

Which value can this situation carry out?

What is a positive thing about this?

I keep asking myself these questions until I think my spirit grows, and my point of view changes. In the course of time, these questions have become a common practice and tend to pop up automatically.

4. Try to be grateful. The most successful people are grateful as usual. Thank you. Be grateful for everything, including what you want in your life; thankfulness makes you happy. It has two advantages, thanks are like a magnet, and it attracts more to be grateful and also opens your mind to a new perspective. Begin your day with appreciation, and from the moment you open your eyes, try to create a mental list of ten things that you are grateful for. Concentrate on being thankful and not just mentioning the items for which you are grateful.

5. Practice Self-acceptance. How often do you beat yourself up about your perceived weakness? Self-acceptance may not always be easy, you strive for a certain body type, but you have no bone structure. It's not your perfect result, be kind to yourself and love your body, even all its imperfections. Self-acceptance is the secret to a positive attitude; only when you are capable of loving and respecting yourself will you be truly happy.

6. Don't leap to conclusions. When a situation goes wrong, it is too easy to judge yourself or others. They often have to accuse someone and make conclusions without considering the evidence. This must be blamed on another person if a person believes that things happen to them and are not the result of any actions taken by them. This is all the product of a negative attitude.

The best way of ending this repetitive blame, jumping to the end of the cycle, is, first of all, to take responsibility for your role and the consequences of your actions. It is also important to take the truth into account concerning a stance or belief on the character of anyone. Seek to understand how another person would have seen these things. Ask yourself what I can know. It is your responsibility to understand, embrace, and learn from what happened.

7. Acknowledging imperfection. I am a recovering perfectionist, acknowledging imperfections. It has been my experience that when things don't go the way I hope or expect, it can be hard to accept. After a lot of practice, I discovered the hope in let things free, might agree that a moment or an occurrence didn't go the way I expected. This new recognition made moving forward and accepting something new and exciting much simpler for me. The transition did not happen immediately, but with practice and time, it has become easier.

8. The most critical action we take was who we get to be around, and we are like the people around us. An old saying says, "show me your friends, and I shall tell you who you are." If they inspire you to pursue your dreams is equally important to consider. Are they positive or negative? Would you promote misery, or do you love to find a new outlook? Let nobody stand in the way that you are the best possible version of yourself and that you create a life you enjoy. Surround yourself with people who are optimistic and similar.

9. Contribute to society. One of the easiest ways to maintain a positive attitude is to volunteer in your neighborhood or in a meaningful manner. Contributing reflects on both others and us, and, therefore, provides a much-needed perspective. As we focus continuously on our own needs and concerns, we increase our issues and lose sight of the larger picture, allowing us to look at the world and the life of others from a different perspective and more often than not, we understand how great things really are, and we become more thankful.

10. Visualization is the secret to a change of mind; it brings us from where we are to concentrate on the result right now. The trick to visualize is to concentrate on the result and how fantastic it is. Visualization with feeling is extremely important, without feeling it is just daydreaming. Visualization is best done every day, usually for about 3 to 5 minutes. Concentrate on what your future will look like with your successes, close your eyes, and breathe deeply. Imagine that you are happy and confident. Do this custom every morning first.

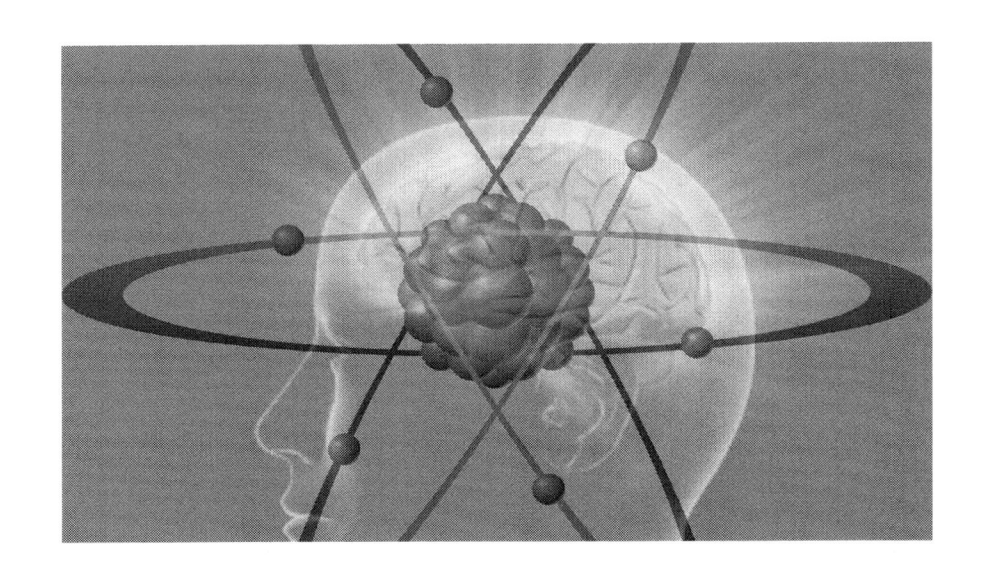

Chapter 8:
Ordinary Consciousness or Mindlessness

When the people asked the Buddha if he were a God, an angel, or a saint, he said, "No, I'm alive." What is Buddha trying to say to us? What are we to wake up from? Why is it more important to be aware?

Normal MINDLESSNESS and CONSCIOUSNESS, a spectrum of perception, is polluted with many harmful patterns of thought, feeling, and reaction in normal consciousness states. These negative patterns are largely unaware of how they prevent us from reaching higher consciousness states. In unconscious states, we are hypnotized; we operate as automatic pilot robots, sleeping through life.

The biggest guilty person is the brain. The undisciplined mind disturbs our lives by bringing us out of today's fullness of our lives. Now, in this place where we learn, enjoy, help others, find our courage, and experience inner peace, the story of life is unfolding.

The undisciplined mind is destroying our unity. The mind takes us out of our present moments again and again when it doesn't like what's happening. He fights when angry, he fights when he is afraid, competes when he is jealous, and creates disasters and fantasies of his desires.

The subconscious is drawn to the past and the future. While learning from the past and hoping for the future is good, the mind goes beyond its replays and projections. We are reviving the wounds, resentments, and regrets of the past, which only recycle rage, disappointment, and guilt. The future projections create unnecessary fear and insecurity.

We construct a rigid structure of selfish, dogmatic, and over-estimated feelings, beliefs, likings, and dislikes. Through manipulating and moving events and people, we try to meet our needs. But the world doesn't adhere to our selfish desires. When things don't suit, we create new desires. Instead of dealing with what we've got, what we think we want next is fantasy. As a consequence, psychological instability and volatile feelings are increased.

The brain is at its best when it understands and functions at a time. It is not built for excesses of attraction, dislike, high emotional reaction, and problem avoidance. All leads to restlessness and speculation, indications that the brain is overheated.

GET SPIRITUAL CONSCIOUSNESS. A former Buddhist practice allows us to control internal responses to an environment of uncertainty and predictability. We want to respond with harmony and calmness, but our thoughts and feelings will not cooperate all too often. Although there can be no escape from challenges and discomfort, concentration allows us to take the tests and tests of life with calm rest. The use of this simple technique allows us to raise our consciousness so that we are awake and ready for anything. By avoiding the destructive excesses of mind and emotion, we can get what life brings with a uniform mind.

In the transformation to spiritual awareness, we can control the mind by placing it where we want it to be awake, attentive, and ready in the current moment. This alignment helps us to understand, solve problems, relax, serve, and enjoy. Through nurturing the testimony as a cure for restlessness and rumination of the mind, we will reach this country.

The witness is a part of the higher self that allows us to experience life's changes with calm neutrality. Improvement is not the witness's goal. We don't insert, erase, delete, or edit. Once we change our frame and mind-set, we accept reality as it is. They reflect on the quiet in and out of the present moment. As the witness grows through the practice of consciousness, the dimensions of space and serenity can gradually be brought into the events of life.

We connect with the flow of destructive and negative thoughts, desires, emotions, visions, and urge that move through our knowledge in ordinary consciousness. With the practice of concentration, they create a space sufficiently large to sustain negative effects. In this vacuum, we do not interact with the rubble and thus need not repress or convey it, which are both harmful. Rather, we go to the compassionate witness of the true self and build a healing room indoors. This is a kind of furnace: here we may burn up the junk thoughts, emotions, desires, and imaginations, which prevent our consciousness from growing.

Love is stronger than any of the roaming powers that cross into our consciousness. Invoking and affirming love and its values, they build a soothing inner environment. When our empathy brings down the disturbing negative, a subsequent change towards harmony and strength takes place.

Aligning the mind and body with the present is a key element in the process of healing. These days, the next step in our spiritual evolution is. We preserve the integrity of our culture, a tale full of lessons, entertainment, and opportunities for making, creating, caring, and serving. Such chances are lost in the lower state of normal consciousness because we are concerned with other consciousness fields.

To practice consciousness, there is no need to alter other than the location of the brain when we perform our usual activities. The mind remains calm and stable in action, regardless of what happens in the material world. We remain in equilibrium. We get the story's flow. There's no energy in it. We're prepared for everything.

TECHNICAL MINDFULNESS Steps:

1. Avoid

2. Start

3. Breathe

4. Present-time

5. Identify Frame:

    a.) Witness

    b.) College

    c.) Entertainment

    d.) Guerrero

    e.) Ritual

6. Repetition

STEP 1: STOP The mind fades into one of its negative behaviors and distracts us from the opportunities of the day. We go on the negative train for a ride. We believe that this is who we are because we identify with the negativity. When we realize that our mind wanders, we stop thinking and concentrate on our breath.

STEP 2: BREATH Take a breath and take your mind back to reality. Through simply knowing our breath, we can avoid the wandering mind and return to the current times of our lives. This easy maneuver that regulates the mind by using our respiration helps us to develop our concentration power. Through constantly taking our attention back to our breath, we build a focused mind each time the mind wanders. With practice, we will remain more and more in the present, getting our mind back into line with the moment.

STEP 3: PRESENT MOMENT. Each moment is given our full attention. We focus on silence within, without the present moment, and on what we do.

STEP 4: FRAME If we use the breath to calm the mind and position it on the current stage, we have a chance to choose from multiple life frames. We can't control most of what happens outside, but we can control how we react. We can choose structures that inspire, cure, relax, purify, entertain, and turn. We can build any frame that we want. We will explore six frames in this lesson: the testimony, class, entertainment, service, the warrior, and ritual.

THE WITNESS

Without reaction, the passive witness watches. The spectator looks at events from a place of calm and harmony. We could invoke the witness with a single breath. Serenity, space, and reflection are here. With the breath as a way of calming ourselves, we will begin to disengage the negative habits of the uncontrolled mind from our identity. We build a peaceful and caring space, instead, large enough to hold anything. Breathe and refocus early and often on the quiet witness to the happiness and joy that lies there, interrupted only by our undisciplined thinking.

EDUCATION

Education is Life. Students in their school life study their inner self and its complexities. Conscious introspection allows us to see the power affecting us. We can understand each other better by constantly watching our feelings, emotions, aversions, urges, fantasies, flow, and impulses. We see how our impulses, Insecurities, and fears cause tension, and how we can release ourselves into space, rhythm, and serenity using the technique of consciousness.

We try to get away when life is hard inside or outside. We resist or escape into unconsciousness or imagination. But the school of life is just a lesson to be learned. In the moments of our lives, the teacher and lessons are found. By learning from them, we cannot pass up the chain of consciousness, and we can't learn if we're not in school: alive, alert, and centered.

Allowing your mind to drift through the school is comparable to playing hooky. Of honesty, we don't fight or run with the teacher. We are patient, listening, and collaborating to progress to the next level. Peace is not achieved by running away. They then find peace by meeting and going through the dilemma or challenge. We should reach through the air instead of running out of displeasure. Through approaching the present profoundly, we will understand and proceed.

The goal is to remain calm and suffer simultaneously. We can do this if we build enough space to cure problems or pain. We can then allow our painful issues to exist without the harmful aspects of denial, suppression of speech in our conscience.

Denial and denial force our debilitating issues into the unconscious and into the body, where negative energy is processed. The problem remains unsolved and secret. Our suffering is expressed in destructive manifestations in so many ways, including power and control over others, irritability, anger, and aggression. We actually spread our pain and concerns to others.

Instead, an inner curative environment for pain can be created. We can do so by invoking ourselves affirmations about compassion, kindness, acceptance, and forgiveness. We create a favorable healing climate, which is greater than any pain or problem. We will learn from our dilemma and disseminate the burden by being polite, compassionate, and gentle with ourselves.

In an expanded, calm, and caring environment, our pain and problems release negative energy that has been repressed over the years in our unconscious and body. Through acknowledging pain and empathy issues, we end the anxiety that anger will be released. The stress of oppression dissolves by stopping the fight inside.

There is a profound sense of peace as we approach our pain without giving resistance. We achieve intimate strength by fully accepting the unavoidable misery of life without oppression and resistance. Whether we reach our suffering with gentleness and bravery, we gain the wisdom and energy to face the next set of problems or lessons. This is pain management by giving up.

To switch our gear from normal to higher, we need to think less, to be aware of our actions, to stay in the present, and to take pain as our instructor. Stay calm, be kind and gentle, and do the job. The effect is power, serenity, room, and silence.

ENTERTAINMENT

The drama of life does not always include college and education. ENTERTAINMENT Life is fun. Life is entertainment. Our stories are full of beauty, happiness, laughter, and fun. Nevertheless, life cannot be treated as entertainment, if we are absorbed in the drama, overwhelmed by our struggles and misery.

We can take ourselves less seriously by taking a step back from the role we play. This is achievable by portraying life as a film or a sport. We are a role player, participants in a game. We gain distance and perspective by not fully identifying ourselves with our position. Once we are, through our propensity to overstate the significance of events, some cognitive restlessness and emotional reactivity are reduced. When we relax the mind and create more space for our activities, we will enjoy the show.

SERVICE

The practice of thoughtfulness helps one overcome the power of negative thoughts and volatile emotions. It allows us to function with the sense of love and service, satisfying our innate desire to nourish everyone who has come with compassion, kindness, and joy. Graceful, warm, and loving service to all humanity and nature is a natural effect of continued consciousness practice.

WARRIOR

The practice of consciousness gradually replaces unrestrained emotions, feelings, and impulses with serenity and calmness instead mental reactivity and restlessness. With a stronger and more robust mentality, life's challenge is less likely to throw us back. We can deal with anything that comes and holds our ground. We don't have to run or hide. We can stay right now, stand, and stand. We are conscious and ready for work, pain, transition, and even unexplained death. This is a religious warrior's place.

RITUAL

We spend times in daily routine activities: cooking, walking in the park, talking on the telephone, lining up, running to the store, cutting grass, washing dishes, baking, tying shoes, brushing teeth and in these patterns of life, there is a sense, but we lack it. Because we believe that the natural is dull, and hence, the mind wanders. At every moment, anywhere, outside and inside, we lose touch with wonder and miracles.

The practice of consciousness gives the life practices reverence by reflecting on our actions and establishing a sense of special significance and value. For example, by understanding the omniscience that is always with us, we can enjoy moments that might otherwise be lost to boredom.

Omniscience is the infinite intelligence that pervades our body and the whole universe. When we do any daily task, if we ask what to do, we should think of how our body follows our orders. We should think about the intelligent wisdom that produces and functions our vision and hearing as we conduct our tasks. When we read, we can think of the brilliance we can understand these words now. As we feed, we should think of how the intestines and the belly digest food by splitting it into molecules sent to the right place in the body to provide fuel, repair, immunity, and many other functions. We can think about how the body responds to our commands while washing our skin.

The wisdom that the body produces and performs is amazing. We are magicians, performing amazing achievements all day long, but ordinary knowledge makes the wonderful worldly stuff. To remain conscious of the universe's omniscience is part of the capture of the marvel, magic, and mystery of being alive, which could otherwise appear to be the stupidity of everyday routines. We can start such a practice anytime, any time and place. We can find them by actively looking for the good inside and outside. A hidden gift lurks everywhere; we just have to work to discover it. If we bring the full power to our routine activities with a calm, concentrated, and positive mind, we can capture the blessings and give them our property.

As we feed, we should think of how the intestines and the belly digest food by splitting it into molecules sent to the right place in the body to provide fuel, repair, provide immunity, and many other functions. We can think about how the body responds to our commands while washing our skin.

The wisdom that the body produces and performs is amazing. We are magicians, performing amazing achievements all day long, but ordinary knowledge makes the wonderful worldly stuff. To remain conscious of the universe's omniscience is part of the capture of the marvel, magic, and mystery of being alive, which could otherwise appear to be the stupidity of everyday routines.

We can start such a practice anytime, any time and any place. We can find them by actively looking for the good inside and outside. A hidden gift lurks everywhere; we just have to work to discover it. If we bring the full power to our routine activities with a calm, concentrated, and positive mind, we can capture the blessings and give them our property. With a breath, focus, and imaginative framing, we can pull the blessings of life from the most mundane activities: love, happiness, elegance, and the magic of being.

STEP 5: REPEAT this takes years to control the brain. Wait for him to switch from the current moment into his old bad habits. Do not regard this as success and failure as frustration and tension. If you ride the thinking train and find yourself in a lower state of consciousness, remain compassionate, understanding, and gentle with yourself. Stop, breathe, and re-enter the moment with your chosen frame.

STEP 6: ONE CONTINUOUS SACRED RITUAL practically, at every time of our lives, we can become more conscious, wakeful, and attentive. When our will strength and focus expand, we will start to merge the moments. Through keeping our attention on what we do all the time, we learn to stay more and more in the moment, even when life is difficult. We can see whether it's good, bad, or ugly.

If we understand that such moments are all we have, that there is no place to go, we gain strength and peace. With a highly developed focus, we can stay in the moment and preserve peace and equilibrium regardless of what life does. Both our moments are part of a continuous cycle, with all its sadness, beauty, and happiness, in answer to the reality of life as it is.

When we control the unruly mind by means of conscience, we gain access to the calm testimony, the school graduate, the actor in the film, the humanity servant, and the warrior ready for anything. The observer remains uniform under all conditions. Life is college when it is hard and painful. We join our suffering to learn the lessons we need. When life is enjoyable, it's like a movie or a game. When we frame life as a movie, we watch or play a role. It gives us a certain perspective and defense against over -implication. Playing with life as if it were a game or a sport lightens our burden. We're not so adamant about it. We are on duty to help others. We think of peace and happiness. The warrior is all set. The ritual transforms the ordinary and the earthly into sacred and special. As we switch these heads, life becomes an on-going sacred ritual, offering its knowledge and learning, entertainment and joy, love and service opportunities.

How to Stop Taking on Negativity from Others

Some students have recently been wondering whether they can drain stress from the people they bring energy and healing to. Nothing in the cycle of spiritual healing, allows you to take in their negative energy, but some people have developed a habit of sponging stuff out of others. But they don't just do it when they do healings or give energy work or counseling, they do it everywhere - with their families, at a party, in the grocery store, so they might also do it when they advise or support people.

In childhood, over-empathy usually begins with the child being naturally hypersensitive. Feeling what others think is a natural gift with which all babies are born, but if early life is difficult, it can turn into a defense mechanism to understand if to get out of the way, or a way to know how to join in, satisfy others, and feel safe. If the child develops a fearful or defensive vibration, it is increasingly possible to perceive incoming information as scary.

Because our vibration draws more of what we vibrate, a spiral often occurs. Whether Life gets more frightening and worse, or it gets better and happier. It's not reality, and it's the creation of each individual psychic or channelers saying things that are frightening, apocalyptic - that are their reality, not yours. A "guides" are felt through the low vibration filter. Your vibration must be high to hear the pure Source, which means that in your life, you are happy and doing well.

Being sensitive is a blessing, but any gift that is taken to the full is a curse. Every force brought to the extreme is a weakness. A temporary reading is supposed to be the gift of attention to what other people feel. Take the reading and then let the feeling go. Try not to bear it for them or take it for them.

But "over empaths" get an exaggerated sense of responsibility for the emotions and well-being of other people. They don't allow others to take responsibility for their own Life and vibration. It's a way to try to control other people or Life.

Feel this if you're an overeater: saving, protecting, transporting, or even handling others isn't your task. The, "wounded healer," is sacrificing herself to support others, and eventually, it is not helping her, and she is not serving her clients as well as she can.

The wounded healer is an extremely "old-paradigm," and it is not advised to be one. Wounded healers should unconsciously be pleased with their sacrifice, and they unintentionally take on that stereotype. You have so much more pleasure in delivering your service without compromising your health and well-being!

If you are sad, always looking for something, broken, exhausted, overweight, out of shape, and unhealthy as a helping man, your first job is to work fabulously for yourself and your future. You need to tap in before you can enable others to tap ineffectively. Get happy, safe, light, and successful and you will want what you have, of course. Live it and show it in your everyday life, and they're going to flock to you. They're gathering the pulse.

Model what you want them to have if you're going to help others.

Signs of over-empathy include: Weight gain - taking on the weight of the world, or your body trying to shield it from what you're forcing it to endure. Fatigue - lack of clarity, confusion, or overwhelming. Depression–Anger;

being attached to how well your customers are doing. Sadness, feelings of the victim, feeling unloved, and giving so much love, yet not receiving it back. Unhappy Life—not taking care of things. We recommend that everyone avoid over-empathy, especially if they are going to provide professional assistance to people in any way.

It's just a vibrational habit, and you can stop working on yourself or doing any particular tasks without analyzing your childhood. You plan to do this in the here and now, where everything is your strength. Sure, low vibrations of the youth can increase, but the "work" of the old paradigm is not involved.

Consider stopping over-empathizing so strongly, and instead; let the Divine do the heavy lifting.

The first thing to do to stop over-empathizing is to make a solid decision: "I'm going to stop carrying on the stress of other people, feel my OWN emotions, get comfortable and mind my own business." If you can't stop it, get individual support.

Second, if we've picked up a bit of low vibration (we're human): Prostrate (lie on the floor face down with your hands lying in prayer position over your head) and put it all down at the feet of The Presence, which is what it does. That's all you have to do. You don't have to be surrounded by white light or do anything to remove it.

People sitting with a popular teacher in a robust and high resonance field get a valuable opportunity to align with it (even from all over the world while listening to audios), which helps them gradually move from their old lower vibrational range to a higher vibrational range. When they do this and let go of BOTH, miracles occur. If I did not let go as a teacher, I would be in the way. If they don't let go yet, there aren't any miracles, however.

If they're not going to let go, it's not my business. If I'm not going to let go, that's my responsibility.

If they've not spoken to me and asked for help, as in cases with family or friends, it's not my business, and I'm going to let go. My role is to love them, not repair them, and enjoy them.

If it's too large for you, just like anywhere else in Life, lay it down—give it to The Presence.

To feel "significant" or unique, or to be on a special mission, some people need to be a healer or helper. If this is you, quickly fix it, as there is the most excellent excuse, regardless of what you are doing. You're on a slippery slope if you need people to make you essential or to say you're powerful. It never succeeds in fulfilment.

Someone who needs help from an educator or therapist has temporarily forgotten who he or she is, and the goal is to reassure them, and they don't need the instructor as soon as possible. There is a hole inside you if you need to be heard, and you seek your fullness by going into The Presence, not helping others.

You might think, "Okay, I'm taking on their issues or problems because I love them, care about them, and have empathy for them." But that doesn't help them. Holding someone's dream as shattered, helpless, poor, and having to repair them continually makes you a contributor to the problem. Sadly, it is often your fear and lack of allowing you to control the flow and goodness of nature and try to carry others and manipulate the beautifully organized World. Learn how things work, and you're going to love it!

Jesus didn't see people as sick or insane, so in his presence, they couldn't be ill or mad for long. His pulse, being divine, has failed a few times, hence his crucifixion. In extreme circumstances, he regained his equanimity on the altar! He is not meant to be an excellent example of martyrdom, as proposed by Christian theology. His message was love and grace—redeeming it without paying any cost.

Others say they are so anxious that they will not be able to go out in crowds. That's just a sign. Their movement is erratic, and they're not able to control it. You can learn how to manage it. It is the one thing you can and ought to control in the Universe—yourself. One, who is rooted, centered, and has set clear goals won't be significantly disturbed by the vibrations of other people.

When you vibrate strongly with the low vibration of someone else, this means that within you, there is a slight hum of that vibration that attracted it. This means allowing you to assess your outside vibrations, rather than the other way around. If not, a low vibration would not resonate with you, or at all stick to you. You'd bop through it happily.

If you like to use your sensitivity to gather useful information, as I do, then let it go every time you get helpful and uplifting information, enjoy it and rave about it.

When you think somebody's negativity, says, "It's not mine, and although I say," yes and thank you for the data' to it, it has to go on." That's how you prepare your machine to do what you want. Practice everywhere, all the time until you get the new habit from your body. It's easy to do.

Low vibrational customer information isn't really who they are.

Believe it not, be interested in it, be emotional about it, or be attached to it.

Programming Your Subconscious Mind

In this reprogram section on the human condition; we discuss briefly the subconscious mind and how its internal workings have a positive and a negative impact on our lives. Also, we explore and establish several practical steps to reprogram our lives and those of the people around us. Through exploring the role that this enigmatic part of our brain plays in defining our very form, we can understand better why we react in certain ways at all times.

In addition to the fundamental aspects of exploring the influential effects of our subconscious mind on our worldviews and behaviors, they will also provide important systemic measures and processes to alter the subconscious to improve every aspect of our lives. Through better knowledge of and effect on the inner working of our minds, we will be better equipped to rise above mediocrity and to live a life of more astonishment and glory. Let us always be clear - consciousness coincides with an awakening event that catapults the person into new, unknown perceptive realities. And when we try to change unconscious conditioned reactions to life, which can affect what we experience at any given moment. Yes, consciousness is the mechanism for beginning the proverbial "wake-up call."

I assume that the core of our current world paradigm shift is an awakening that is virtually empty of the ego's power. One might say that the on-going planetary spirit we are now playing is a coalescing of the various aspects of the human psyche generated by our collective responses to the whole of life. Now we seem to be combining split minds, souls, and ego with our divine self into a fully formed, "truer" individual. If we can agree on that basic premise, we must also recognize the influential role of our subconscious mind that drives our thinking process and behavior, which can fuel another influential dimension of the ego itself.

While we are frail people, we don't have to demonize the role and value of the ego in life but understand that the sub-conscious is a primary source of fuel that contributes partly to the breathing of life into the ego. In the sense of psychology, there is an idea, that our personal identities are closely linked to our egos, and existence is often guided unconsciously in many different ways only by our ego, and not necessarily by our divine, higher, or true spiritual nature, without realizing this relation. Within this paradox, it can be difficult to detach from a more comprehensive view of the interrelationship of all life unknown. This is a rational account of the false impression of separation and or disconnection.

Life can be a confounding vortex of dominant energies and thought-forms—conscious, egoistic, lower, etc., which seem to dissolve into chaotic dance, leading, and following each other while living music plays on. Luckily, music is now becoming simpler, more synchronous, and harmonious with each day, making personal changes easier to detect and are more adaptable.

What is the Unconscious Mind?

The brain is literally divided or split into two entities, the conscious and the unconscious part. The conscious part of your mind is now active in its primary operation when you read these words to assimilate their meaning. The unconscious consumes and gathers this data in parallel fashion as well as "under the radar," another part of your brain, which creates its own assumptions based on historical sources stored in a configured, perception, or consciousness archive.

While working tirelessly behind the scenes under your conscious knowledge, this incredibly and enormously powerful part of our make-up is, in many ways, responsible for how we react to every aspect of life. Each event is categorically logged into the unconscious continuously and automatically without fail, just as a dry sponge can absorb fluid. It does not deny something. One amazing fact is that all this knowledge -gathering starts in our earliest days - at childhood - and never stops. For example, why are children so impressive? Know no more. Guess no more. The sub-conscious mind of a child is almost blank because of minimal experiences in life that give it a point of reference and eventually influence the conscious mind of decision-making.

The same can be said for people who have little familiarity with life-changing events or access to thought-provoking abstract ideas for whatever reason. One of the main reasons for this special feature is that it functions as much as cruise control or an autopilot deep inside the body. Due to this collection and assimilation process, the subconscious mind fills up a repository quickly and continuously and gains strength and power by offering answers to the present activity generated by the conscious or awakened mind. The cross-conduct of mental tasks between the two minds constitutes a completely natural phenomenon and is representative of a healthy mind under normal mental conditions.

The unconscious part of the brain is an enigmatic aspect of our psychological structure at first. However, as we just read, part of the reason it seems elusive and inaccessible stems mainly from its operational process. The influential power of the subconscious mind is to direct our lives without us fully comprehending its existence or influence in life. Most people do not understand any of their actions and, therefore, have trouble understanding the meaning or the importance that our subconscious mind provides because we normally cannot reach this special place in our minds. Instead, we do not have the resources or knowledge necessary to produce improvements to its content in the absence of information.

When the subconscious mind controls our thoughts and actions unconsciously, through the programming instructions or language it works from through our accumulated creeds, life experiences, and worldviews around us, we can actively rewrite our unconscious thoughts, through advanced training, to gain more control over our lives.

Why is the unconscious re-programmed?

Taking this broad, influential, and powerful aspect of our mind into account and appreciating it, most of us would prefer a life that continually evolves positively, benefiting us and, as a normal by-product, the well-being of others. Once this noble desire is understood in reality, the consequences for improving all of life are ultimately profound, since we will become naturally interrelated.

Through cohesively linking the two minds and understanding their experiences, we will begin to reprogram parts of our subconscious mind, which are responsible for the self-sabotaging of our strongest, highest expectations and desires. In everyday life, we often experience repeated but hidden symptoms in our sub-consciousness that prevent us from experiencing our highest purpose as more happiness, productivity, success, and healthy living. It is at this point that we are becoming aware of something that affects our actions and determines the best intentions to resolve these conflicts within us.

This is the watershed moment of great opportunity! The best examples of these deeply hidden symptoms caused by the subconscious are those with a significant emotional energy "memory signature." One such example is that you feel rejected by someone you care about or love. In the next scenario with a perceived rejection potential, our conscious mind will soon obtain a built-in inference from the unconscious to explain the denial. Although this is a false assumption, you may unconsciously deny any likelihood of full acceptance that another person or circumstance can give in advance. The same applies to intense, emotionally charged, low-self-esteem disputes, which happen when you have encountered insufficiency, assumed failure, or when someone assumes or labels you incompetent, useless, lazy, or sometimes even worse!

Some of all negative connotations impart very vivid imagery that, if off conscious or inconsistent, in several aspects of your life will contribute to a lifelong battle cycle. Reprogramming your unconscious against negatively charged embedded responses is not hard when you are willing to implement some simple procedures that will strengthen your mental balance and outward reaction to life as a whole over time.

The How to

Luckily for those who want to change things, some validated methods are available to reprogram the subconscious mind successfully. Such strategies replace undesirable reactions by substituting them in the depth of the brain with specific or more constructive stimuli within the body.

Through time a matching response was expected and viewed as a reaction to conscious thoughts generated in waking life. The unconscious programming did not evolve over the night. Taking this into account, it is important to note that these approaches are exponentially more efficient by continuous application and yield quick results. Five successful (and advanced) methods are given below to start the reprogramming process.

Visualization

The unconscious responds to visual stimuli very well. Seeing images that generate love, happiness, and gratitude that make you emotionally satisfied can create positive images within the unconscious as if you witnessed them physically. The unconscious cannot distinguish between reality and the fictional, as only feelings are affected. Collect pleasant images from all sources you see to induce positive feelings. Repetition of the presentation of these images means that actual memories are not required and can be told anywhere in mind at any time.

Affirmations

There is no easier way in the unconscious to deliver positive messages. Make simple claims that are NOT rendered in the present context. For example, "I am" instead of "I will." Only the present moment for the unconscious makes no sense for the future. This is a very important difference. Coincide terms with corresponding thoughts and pictures in the positive sentence. Repetitive repetition is the key to success with well-formed sentences so that you can communicate them verbally and internally anywhere. If done correctly, they are very effective.

Environmental impact

Many claim that we represent the organization or atmosphere that we sustain. Everyone lives the reality they expect. It's true. External encounters with objects, places, or activities can also have a positive or negative impact on the subconscious mind. Your best guide is to reconcile with your conscious mind and heart, an acceptable emotional response to the external influence, irrespective of your initial emotional response. If faced with potentially unwanted encounters, for example, filter your answer by searching for something positive about the case. Remain focused on all the positive aspects, so that a negative response or harmful effect can be neutralized.

Hypnosis

Here is a scientifically validated approach that has withstood the test of time and has enormous potential to offer assistance in an appropriate setting. Hypnosis may begin unconscious reprogramming under a trained practitioner, essentially bypassing the conscious, filtering portion of one's mind. This short-cut saving time approach is very useful for many because it easily shifts actions by implanting specific changes or statements of belief in the subconscious. One usually looks for a well-trained hypnosis specialist to facilitate customized sessions for performance.

Brain Entrainment

Another popular method with similar effects to hypnosis without the need of a hypnotist is a mental exercise. Write of yourself-hypnosis. Modern science has shown special, variable levels in our brains while in different mental states. If one were to make, in one of those specific brain frequencies, nearly inaudible persuasive comments or optimistic declarations such as those present during deep meditation, shifts in the subconscious could be quickly realized. Once again, repeating the use of this approach is very important. Several good sources of brain training audios are widely available, most of which are meant to target specific changes in the unconscious. Equally important, many learning audios are well crafted because they are combined with fun soundtracks.

Reprogramming Checklist

There are 17 light points to be recalled, perceived, and applied habitually, thus triggering necessary modifications of your sub-consciousness. This is indeed a lifestyle and a noble business that offers you rich personal and worldly rewards. Below are some well-known and less well-known, easily implemented thoughts and acts to help you improve a new one! Check out what resonates and find (no matter if positive or negative) what these emotions are when you study the list. This dramatic reply gives you useful, emotionally focused insights into the things that improve your life as soon as they are implemented. Your superior person is always your best guide. Now, that little voice will never deceive you. Recognize this superior, impartial advice and make phenomenal changes in all areas of your life. As they say, it's good to take an examination periodically from the chest.

Believe in yourself first and foremost.

Understand what holds you off to conquer it.

Spend time at least once a day in quiet self-reflection, prayer, or meditation.

Put all in and out of your mind.

Know in very specific terms what you want.

Remove all negative influences from your life.

Surround yourself with people who are positive and successful.

Create a realistic plan to achieve your deepest wishes.

Take positive steps every day to attract what you want.

Focus on the present—as if you've received what you want already.

Create visual memories of your objectives and intentions.

Please record your favorite claims or order a self-hypnosis DVD.

By matching your feelings to your desires, avoid conflicting messages.

Write a newspaper report on your performance as if it happened already.

Be your advocate and grant praise and compliments.

Choose to be positive at all times. Have a thanksgiving disposition.

Conclusion

By closing, let us not overpower the conscious mind in all this. It also has a valuable role to play in transforming our often-illusory subconscious mind. One of the best and worthy of note is that we are conscious of both our own thoughts and reactions to everyday life with all its apparent distractions. The conscious part of our mind as a proverbial gatekeeper could easily be imagined.

Although simplistic as it may seem, for those of us who want more joy in life, simplicity is necessary and should not be left out of this courageous effort. Use and enlist the help of the left logical part of your brain, while not lacking the intuitive power of the right brain. By doing this, you have a strong, up-to-date ally ready to track and support you.

Enable your conscious mind to recall your thoughts and responses even in your daily activities. Through actively tuning your thoughts as it happens, it is an important key that eventually produces the type of outcomes you need.

By just a few realistic and aware implementations of what you have learned, this will become second nature and open the doors to a more productive redirection of thoughts that spill into the unconscious. In short, you and those around you can see actual improvements and related changes visually.

First of all, recognize and thank yourself for reading this because it testifies to the will and to the desire to be a more awake human being. We're all on this journey together, so be simple and easy on your own. Remove cognitive control, which sometimes follows any challenge to unnecessary predisposed ego responses from the subconscious.

Note that the entire process is not difficult and that it takes you time to permeate and alter your unconscious for the better. Just decide to participate voluntarily and start the process. And don't forget, it's great too since we have eternity to achieve perfection!

Made in the USA
Monee, IL
21 September 2021